Chafing Dish & Fondue Cook Book

By the Editors of Sunset Books and Sunset Magazine

LANE BOOKS • MENLO PARK, CALIFORNIA

Edited by Jan Thiesen

Special Consultant: Annabel Post
HOME ECONOMICS EDITOR,
SUNSET MAGAZINE

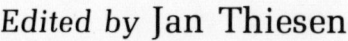

Illustrations: Henry Rasmussen

Design: Lawrence A. Laukhuf

Cover: Swiss Cheese Dipping Sauce, page 26.
Photographed by George Selland, Moss Photography.

Photographers: Glenn Christiansen: page 36. Norman A. Plate: page 7.
Darrow M. Watt: pages 4, 10, 22, 46, 66.

Second Printing August 1971

Copyright © Lane Magazine & Book Company, Menlo Park, California. First Edition 1971. World rights reserved. No part of this publication may be reproduced by any mechanical, photographic, or electronic process, or in the form of a phonographic recording, nor may it be stored in a retrieval system, transmitted, or otherwise copied for public or private use without prior written permission from the publisher. Library of Congress No. 70-141178. Title No. 376-02281-7.
Lithographed in the United States.

Contents

4   AN INTRODUCTION TO TABLE TOP COOKING

10   APPETIZER ARTISTRY... USING TABLE TOP COOKWARE

22   FONDUE... WITH CHEESE, OIL, BROTH

36   SAUCES... SAVORY ACCENTS TO COMPLEMENT FONDUE

46   CHAFING DISH ENTREES... ELEMENTARY TO ELEGANT

66   DESSERTS... PREPARED AT THE TABLE

80   INDEX

Orange-liqueur-accented Strawberries Fire and Ice (page 69) are ladled flaming over ice cream.

An Introduction to Table Top Cooking

When you think about *good* restaurants and *fine* food, visions of elegantly-outfitted waiters effortlessly preparing flambéed masterpieces probably come to mind.

If you're like most cooks, at one time or another you've wanted to duplicate this same technique, which seems so effortless, at home. And no wonder. These performances, put on with such finesse, are fascinating to watch.

More informal than elegant, fondue is particularly appropriate for people who consider conversation and companionship as important as the food itself. Guests do their own dunking or cooking at the table, and dining is done at a leisurely pace (more specific information begins on page 23).

To make cooking at the table satisfying for you and impressive—and fun—for your friends, there are certain basics you need to know about equipment, fuel, organization, and safety that apply to both chafing dish and fondue cooking.

Equipment

Good equipment helps to insure successful cooking at the table. There are many table cooking units available today, and some are more versatile than others. When selecting new equipment, consider first the kinds of table cooking you want to do. If you can own more than one unit, a traditional chafing dish (described on page 47) and a fondue bourguignonne pan (discussed below and in more detail on page 28) might be your choices. By adding pans of different shapes (such as a wide, shallow pan for flaming crêpes and an earthenware casserole for cheese fondue), you could prepare almost any recipe in this book.

You might prefer to buy a single portable table top burner that can accommodate a variety of pans, and you may find that you have appropriate pans on hand that are attractive enough to use at the table. Electric fondue pots are another possibility. Many styles are available, and most are designed to cook a wide variety of dishes.

In deciding pan sizes, consider the number of guests you normally entertain and the type of entertaining you most often do. For example, a pan of 2-quart capacity might hold the main dish for 2 to 6 people or appetizers for as many as 20.

Crêpes Suzette Pan. This wide, shallow pan (typically about 10 inches wide and 1 inch deep) is designed for flaming crêpes at the table. Its shape shows off the flames well and makes it easy to baste crêpes while they are being flamed. This pan is also ideal for quick sautéing of meat, fish, eggs, and fruit, or for any cooking that calls for high, direct heat. Choose a good heavy pan of a metal that conducts heat well to accomplish even heating and good browning. Any attractive frying pan can substitute for a crêpes suzette pan.

Earthenware Fondue Pot. This classic dish is flameproof and comes in several sizes, usually ranging from 1 to 3-quart capacity. It is traditionally used for cheese fondue, but it can also be used for heating and serving casseroles, stews, or soups. When used over a direct flame, it gives an even, low heat. Any similarly shaped flameproof casserole of glass ceramic, ceramic material, or heavy metal can be substituted for this pot. (More information begins on page 24.)

Fondue Bourguignonne Pan. A vessel of many uses, this pan, usually 1½ or 2-quart capacity, has inward-sloping sides that help prevent spattering when cubes of meat on forks or skewers are cooked in hot oil. By regulating the heat, this container may also be used for cheese fondue, keeping sauces or gravies warm, and for preparing many desserts and dessert sauces in the chapter beginning on page 67.

Electric Fondue Pots. Several styles are available. Most units can be regulated to give the right heat for cheese, oil, broth, and dessert fondues, and can be used for heating and serving other foods as well. These units have the obvious advantage of keeping heat automatically at the proper temperature. Since there is no open flame, these containers have a safety advantage over other burners.

Fuels For Cooking and Warming

No matter what kind of fuel you use—some authorities recommend one, others rely exclusively on another, still others use them interchangeably—high heat is essential for some main courses cooked at the table, such as meats that require quick browning.

The recipes in this book call for a wide range of cooking temperatures, from high heat for browning or cooking foods to very low heat for keeping foods at the correct serving temperature. To help you decide which fuels to use, here are some considerations.

Alcohol Burners. These come in a number of styles, but in two general categories: wick and compressed fiber. You regulate the flame by lengthening or shortening the wick on the first, and by opening or closing a damper (controlling the amount of air) on the second. The size of the alcohol container determines how long it will burn before refueling is necessary. *Never add fuel until the flame is completely out and the burner is cool* (see the information on "Safety" on page 9).

Denatured alcohol is usually recommended for use in alcohol burners, but the less expensive isopropyl (rubbing) alcohol may be used. The two fuels have vastly different heating powers; denatured alcohol burns with a much hotter flame and should be used when actual cooking is required. Isopropyl alcohol may be used when you merely wish to keep a dish hot.

To obtain maximum amount of heat with alcohol burners, the unit should be designed so that the cooking pan, when resting on the stand, is not more than 2 inches from the source of heat.

Canned Heat Burners. These units consist of a stand with a holder for canned heat. The holder has a lid-like piece with a handle with which you can increase or decrease the size of the flame. Some units hold a large can (7 oz.), but most home units are designed for a small can (2⅜ oz.). A small can will last from 45 to 60 minutes and a large can from 4 to 5 hours.

Canned heat burns with a somewhat cooler flame than denatured alcohol. Some canned heat units are designed with a shield which goes from the base to the top of the stand to cut down heat loss. And when a heat shield is used, and provided the cooking pan, resting on the stand of the unit, is no more than 2 inches from the heat source, these burners give comparable heat to alcohol burners.

By partially covering the can opening, the canned heat may be controlled, such as when you want to lower the heat to keep foods warm.

Butane Burners. Single and double butane burners are available. This burner most resembles a gas range; heat is controlled simply by adjusting the flame. This is an excellent choice for preparing dishes that require quick-cooking and high heat, such as Steak Diane.

Candle Heating Units. These units consist of a stand and special candle holder. Fireproof casseroles or pans can be placed on the stand, and many of these units come with a casserole. Candles can also be set inside canned heat units.

The candle (buy one designated for warming) should be used only for keeping cooked foods warm. The flame is not hot enough for actual cooking, and its heat is too slow to be practical for heating foods to a serving temperature. Advantages of this type of heating unit are that most warming candles burn for about 3 hours, you do not have to worry about adding more fuel in the middle of a dinner or party, and it will not overcook the food. It is also very inexpensive.

Convertible Burners. There are some units available that will use either alcohol or canned heat. These are generally sold as a separate stand which will accommodate almost any kind of pan for cooking. Candles may also be used, but the burner should be lightly lined with aluminum foil to eliminate possible cleaning problems.

Restaurant Units. Restaurants often use special heating units and pans that are designed to provide more heat and better heat control than the average piece of equipment available in housewares stores. Although quite expensive—these

Samples of typical table top cooking equipment include: Top row, left to right, portable butane burner with heat adjustment in the handle; traditional alcohol-burning chafing dish; electric fondue-tempura pan. Middle row: convertible burner which uses either liquid alcohol or canned heat; classic metal fondue pot; electric fondue-and-mini-frying pan combination. Bottom row: earthenware cheese fondue pot; double burner; alcohol burner with wick.

INTRODUCTION 7

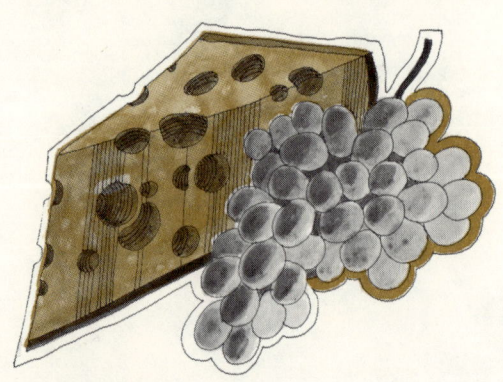

burners can be purchased through restaurant supply stores.

Other equipment that can be used for table top cooking includes regular frying pans placed over small hibachis (best done outside for adequate air circulation), the large alcohol-fueled chafing dish burner, and, for absolute simplicity and security, an electric frying pan.

Pyrotechniques . . . the Art of Flaming Foods

Producing flaming foods is actually a simple scientific procedure that once understood is readily mastered. But to the uninitiated, there are a number of questions as to how to begin and what to do.

There are two reasons for flaming foods. The first is the obvious one of showmanship; setting a fire draws attention and creates undeniable dramatics. The second reason is more subtle, but also more important: the delicate flavor essence that remains once the alcohol burns away.

The flammability of a liqueur is directly related to its alcoholic content, and somewhat related to its sugar content. Any liqueur containing 20 per cent (40 proof) alcohol or more can be induced to catch fire (to determine per cent, divide the proof rating in half); this includes most Sherries, vermouths, and Madeiras, and such flavored liqueurs as Kahlua, creme de menthe, or creme de cacao. Additionally, there are the beverages usually considered for flaming—rum, brandy, kirsch, and all the others that are 80 to 151 proof.

The more alcohol a beverage contains the longer it will burn, and liqueurs with sugar content will burn slightly longer than another non-sweet liqueur of the same per cent alcohol.

When you flame a liqueur, you don't actually burn the alcohol, you burn the fumes. To release enough fumes to start a fire, you need to heat the liquid quickly; many people have trouble igniting a liqueur because they do not get it hot enough or because they heat it too slowly. The most vigorous fires occur on liqueurs that are actually boiling; if the liqueur is in a shallow pan and held over a flame, it tends to self-ignite.

This is the procedure we recommend: Measure the liqueur into a small, long-handled pan (such as a butter melter or metal measuring cup) and place it on direct heat (a table top burner or a range top) and heat it quickly until bubbling, then hold a burning match close to the surface. The alcohol flame burns blue and is hard to see unless the room is darkened. *Keep face, hands, and clothing away from the flames.*

Pour the burning liqueur at once into or over the foods to be flamed. To maintain the flame and burn off as much alcohol as possible, constantly agitate the mixture by stirring or shaking the pan. If the pan is on heat, and the ingredients bubbling, this creates maximum activity and the flaming will be quite vigorous; keep container in an open area. You will also achieve maximum flaming in a wide shallow pan rather than in a deeper pan.

In some cases you can flame liqueurs once they are mixed with food, but it is tricky and the above method is far more reliable. However, if you are cooking in a small amount of butter or other fat, and there are few juices, you will probably be able to flame the liqueur-fat mixture once it is heated.

Care of Equipment

Before washing, the base of any container and the burner stand should first be wiped with a soft cloth or paper towel to remove the lightly burned-on residue.

Cooled oil should be poured into a jar with a tight-fitting lid, not down the drain. Wipe out any remaining grease with a paper towel, then fill the container with hot soapy water. Use a non-scratching cleaning pad to dislodge the cooked-on oils around the inside edge of the pan. (If you're going to soak the pan completely, remove wooden handles first. If this is not possible, do not immerse the entire pan.)

Copper fondue pots and other pans will need the additional assistance of a commercial copper cleaner.

Before initial use, some manufacturers recommend that you soak the utensil in a special solution (which they suggest) to remove a protective film which inhibits tarnishing. This must be done according to directions, or the container will have a tendency to streak, discolor, and be difficult to polish.

For dissolving cheese, use an all-purpose liquid cleaner which contains ammonia. Forks may be soaked or, if the handles are wooden, swished around in this solution.

Safety

There are certain obvious dangers to cooking at the table.

First, you are using a flammable material, either liquid or solid, as fuel. With meat and fish fondues, you are also dealing with a pot of hotter-than-boiling-water oil.

These factors make it imperative that the subject of table top cooking, or cooking over an open flame, be taken quite seriously—not just for expertise in showmanship, but for your protection as well.

Denatured alcohol is difficult to measure out exactly, although as you become acquainted with your particular unit, you'll have a better idea as to the amount it will safely hold and how long the flame will last.

Do not add too much alcohol when filling the container. Flames may get out of hand.

When pouring the alcohol into the unit, make certain that you do so carefully. It's safest to pour it over the sink so spills don't fall on flooring or furniture. To lessen the chance of flare-ups, wipe the burner carefully with a soft dry cloth before placing it back in the stand.

NEVER add alcohol if the fuel container is still warm. To do so invites a possible explosion. If the flame does go out in the middle of cooking, sip wine, eat salad or bread, or just sit there and talk until the container is completely cool.

If possible, you should always remove the fuel container completely from the base, taking it to the kitchen, again to avoid accidental spills.

IF a flare-up does occur, don't panic. Keep the lid to the container handy and place it back on the pot. If the flames are coming from the fuel, turn off or close the heat unit to smother the flames. Baking soda sprinkled over the area will also smother the flames. (Don't use flour, starch, or baking powder since these are explosive when in the form of a dust.)

Even after careful pouring and wiping, there might be a brief flare-up from fumes. Keep an eye on the fuel container and be handy with the baking soda, but it will probably die down quickly.

Above all, don't try to douse an oil fire with water. This will only make matters worse.

The fondue pot should never be more than half-filled with oil. If the oil level is too high, spattering becomes more apparent and potentially more dangerous.

When heating oil for a meat or seafood fondue, always use a metal fondue pot. Earthenware might not withstand the high temperature and could crack.

Be extremely cautious when carrying the heated oil from the range to the heating unit at the table. It's a good idea to keep small children and pets in another room rather than risk the chance that their curiosity might cause you to trip and fall.

On that same order, oil fondue would also be recommended fare for adults rather than small children. If children are doing their own cooking, make certain that they can reach the container easily.

A second fork should be provided for removing the cooked meat from the boiled-in-oil fondue fork. This is to prevent burning your lips on the hot metal.

Never pour alcohol directly from the bottle into any heated dish. Flames could shoot right back up into the bottle with disastrous results.

A final note . . . These cautions are meant to impress upon you the potential dangers of table top cooking. Some of these problems could just as easily occur in the kitchen under "normal" conditions.

As long as you take some precautions and use common sense, you should have very little, if any, difficulty.

INTRODUCTION

Chunks of salami or proscuitto-wrapped Swiss cheese (page 13) sizzle in oil until slightly melted.

10 APPETIZERS... USING TABLE TOP COOKWARE

Appetizer Artistry... Using Table-Top Cookware

Every hostess enjoys having an ace up her sleeve when it comes to hors d'oeuvres. This course, more than any other, leaves room for experimentation on the part of cook and guests. Almost everyone is willing to try something new when they know it's just a bite and not the entire dinner—in case it isn't a favorite food.

But at the same time, the purpose of an appetizer is to entice and pique the appetite. It should have eye as well as taste appeal. In order to achieve this you should concentrate on a few good combinations rather than spend time on a bevy of so-so selections.

Prior to dinner, one hot appetizer and perhaps a couple of cold ones are usually sufficient. In the case of a cocktail party, however, you will want a variety on hand for nibbling throughout the evening.

And what makes for added interest in the appetizer line? When the gathering is small, friends will undoubtedly be intrigued if they actually *see* you put together a marvelous offering.

In the selection that follows, some appetizers are prepared ahead and kept warm in your chafing dish, fondue pot, or similar vessel; others are partially prepared in the kitchen and finished at the dining table, coffee table, or serving cart. Some are done almost completely before friends.

Bagna cauda, garlicky aïoli, and a traditional Swedish dipping kettle—and any of the fondues beginning on page 23—are do-it-yourself appetizers that can work equally as an entree depending upon accompaniments.

There are a number of dips that hold beautifully. When they are served as an appetizer, just remember to station a pot-watcher alongside since the mixture must be stirred regularly to prevent scorching.

Versatile shrimp are used in a number of ways to make intriguing hors d'oeuvres. Although on the expensive side, they do add a luxury touch that complements other party appetizers.

Mushrooms can be extended beautifully—also in a multitude of ways.

And then there are meatballs—which come in countless variations and seem to appeal to everyone. Made in miniature bite-size balls, they may be kept warm in any kind of table top heating unit—from an electric trivet to a candle warmer to fondue pot—as well as chafing dish or electric frying pan.

Proof that pancakes go from morning to midnight and even beyond is reinforced with the recipe for versatile crêpes and several fillings. Chafing dish or attractive frying pan over low flame will hold them perfectly so they'll remain fresh and warm.

Even beef stew with a minimum of sauce can be held in a fondue pot, chafing dish, or other attractive pan over a portable burner for hearty eating at leisure.

To take as much advantage of your cookware as possible, consider any of your table top cooking equipment for soups, punches, dips, and dunks—for any food that you wish served warm and kept warm over a period of time.

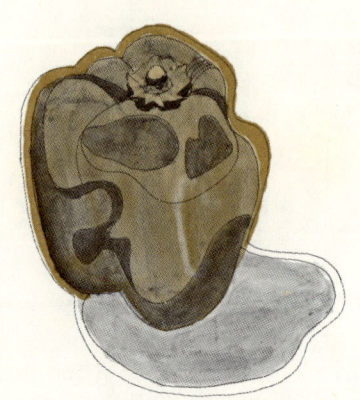

Hot Clam Dip

4 slices bacon, chopped
1 small clove garlic, minced or mashed
1 can (7 oz.) minced clams, undrained
2 teaspoons cornstarch
½ teaspoon basil, crumbled
¼ cup tomato purée
¼ teaspoon salt
⅛ teaspoon pepper
2 teaspoons minced parsley
2 tablespoons grated or shredded Parmesan cheese
Potato chips or hard French rolls

Have all the ingredients on hand and make this hot dip in your chafing dish while guests look on and enjoy the fragrances.

In a chafing dish or electric frying pan, cook bacon and garlic over moderate heat until bacon is crisp and lightly browned. Drain off all but about 2 tablespoons bacon drippings. Bring to the table.

Add clams, blended with cornstarch, basil, tomato purée, salt, pepper, and parsley. Cook, stirring, until mixture is thickened and simmering.

Blend in cheese; keep warm in a hot water bath or over very low heat. (If mixture thickens too much, stir in a little milk.)

Serve as a dip for potato chips or thin slices of hard French rolls or other favorite snack cracker. Makes about 1¼ cups.

Green Chile and Cheese Dip

2 tablespoons salad oil
2 medium-sized onions, chopped
1 tablespoon flour
½ cup regular-strength chicken broth
½ cup sour cream
1 can (4 oz.) California green chiles, chopped (seeds and pith removed)
1 can (4 oz.) pimentos, chopped
3 cups shredded mild Cheddar or Longhorn cheese
Tortilla chips

This cheesy dip can turn out moderate to *hot*, depending on the strength of the chopped green chiles.

In a chafing dish or frying pan combine salad oil and onions; cook, stirring, until soft. Blend in flour. Gradually add broth, then sour cream. Heat until boiling and slightly thickened.

Add chiles and pimentos to sauce, then gradually stir in shredded cheese until melted.

To serve, keep sauce warm over hot water, a candle, or warming tray; scoop onto tortilla chips to eat. Makes 2½ cups or 12 appetizer servings.

Salami and Cheese Fondue

¼ pound thinly sliced beef salami
¼ pound thinly sliced boiled ham
or prosciutto
½ pound natural Swiss cheese
Thinly sliced French rolls
½ cup (¼ lb.) butter
1 cup salad oil

Cubes of natural Swiss cheese overwrapped with slices of salami or prosciutto melt in the mouth after a quick dip in the bubbling hot oil.

Cut salami slices in thirds, lengthwise; cut prosciutto in 1 by 3-inch strips. Cut cheese into ½-inch cubes. Arrange meat strips, cheese cubes, and bread slices in a shallow bowl or on a board.

Heat butter and oil in a deep fondue pot over alcohol flame until foamy. Do not allow fat to brown.

To cook, wrap a meat strip around a cheese cube, spear on a bamboo skewer, and immerse in hot fat until cheese begins to melt. Place on a French roll slice to eat. Makes 8 to 10 servings.

Garlic Pork Nuggets

5 pounds lean pork
1 tablespoon salt
Freshly ground pepper
3 cloves garlic, puréed

Eat these crispy chunks of pork as they are, or dip them in a bowl of taco sauce. Pork shoulder is an especially good cut to use for this dish. This is an easy appetizer to prepare for a crowd, so it is given here in party proportions.

Cut pork into 1-inch cubes; mix thoroughly with salt, pepper, and garlic. Spread in layers in shallow baking pans; bake in a moderate oven (350°) for 1 hour. Stir occasionally and drain off fat accumulations.

When serving, reheat about a pound at a time in the chafing dish over moderately high heat, or reheat in the oven. Serve from chafing dish. Makes enough to serve about 50 people.

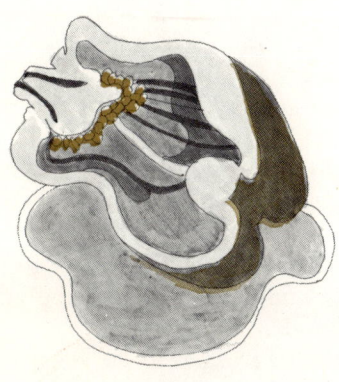

Ajoqueso

1 small can (4 oz.) peeled
green chiles
1 large onion, minced
2 cloves garlic, minced
¼ cup olive oil
2 tablespoons flour
1 cup half-and-half (light cream)
½ pound shredded mild Cheddar or
jack cheese

Here is a garlicky version of Mexican *chile con queso* (chile with cheese). Make it in a fondue pot, chafing dish, or electric frying pan at the table and serve it with corn chips as an appetizer.

Rinse the seeds from chiles and cut into fine dice. Cook onion and garlic in olive oil until wilted. Add flour and stir over direct heat until bubbly, about 2 minutes.

Gradually stir in cream until smooth. Add cheese and the chiles. Heat, stirring, until cheese melts. Transfer, if necessary, to fondue pot or chafing dish, keeping warm over table top burner or water bath. Makes about 8 servings as an appetizer dip (or 4 servings as an entree over toast or tortilla chips).

APPETIZERS ... USING TABLE TOP COOKWARE

Clam and Sausage Appetizers

2 cans (about 8 oz. each) minced clams
1 pound bulk pork sausage
1 egg
2 tablespoons fine dry bread crumbs
⅛ teaspoon pepper
Dill Sauce or Newburg Sauce (recipes follow)

These clam and sausage balls brown neatly and quickly in the oven. Once baked, they're transferred to the chafing dish to keep warm. The Dill or Newburg Sauce adds flavor.

Drain clams, reserving the juices. In a bowl combine the sausage, clams, egg, bread crumbs, pepper, and 2 tablespoons of the reserved clam juice. Mix well, then form into 48 balls about the size of a walnut.

Arrange the clam balls about 1½ inches apart on shallow baking pans. Bake, uncovered, in a 500° oven for 4 minutes. With a spatula turn meatballs over, and cook about 4 minutes longer, until lightly browned.

Using a slotted spoon, lift clam balls out of pans and into a chafing dish. Pour over the Dill or Newburg Sauce and keep warm. Makes 4 dozen.

Dill Sauce: In a small pan heat 1 can (6 oz.) white sauce with ¼ cup of the reserved clam juice, ¼ teaspoon dill weed, and 1 tablespoon Sherry (optional).

Newburg Sauce: Heat 1 can (about 9 oz.) Newburg Sauce with 2 tablespoons of reserved clam juice and 1 tablespoon Sherry (optional).

Bagna Cauda

Bagna cauda (*bag-nyah caw-daw*) is a bold, garlic-and-anchovy-flavored sauce with a butter-and-olive-oil base. Into this blending go a variety of fresh vegetables—but only for a brief dip to flavor, not to cook. Almost any container will work for keeping the sauce hot—from saucepan set over a candle warmer to chafing dish—depending upon the amount made.

This is an adaptable appetizer; from 8 to 30 guests may be accommodated by a simple increase in ingredients.

To keep that fresh-from-the-garden look, vegetables are cut just enough so portions are easy to break away for dipping.

Arrange vegetables in a basket, place alongside the hot butter-oil sauce, and serve with another basket of thinly sliced French bread or crusty rolls.

To eat, swirl a piece of vegetable through the liquid, using either fingers or skewer. Hold a piece of bread beneath to catch drips between sauce and mouth. Eventually the bread soaks up enough drippings to become a tasty morsel in itself.

When figuring amounts, keep in mind that people are often able to consume an astonishing quantity of bagna cauda—it's easy to justify taking your fill of the fresh, crisp vegetables because very little of the rich sauce actually adheres to each morsel.

Bagna Cauda Vegetables

You'll need about 1 to 2 cups vegetable pieces per person, but you'll have to estimate quantities while vegetables are still whole. Choose a colorful assortment. Sprinkle with water just before serving.

Artichokes. Break off small outer bracts; cut thorny tips from remaining bracts with scissors. Trim stem ends. Keep in acid water (1 tablespoon vinegar to 1 quart water) to prevent darkening until ready to serve. To eat, bite off tender base of each bract.

Cabbage. Cut red or white cabbage in half. Cut vertical gashes in each half. Break off chunks to eat.

Carrots. Leave on an inch of stem; peel. Gash carrot not quite through in short sections; break apart to eat.

Cauliflower. Cut out core, keeping head whole. Break off flowerettes to eat.

Cherry tomatoes. Dip with stems.

Green beans. Snap off ends and remove strings. Leave whole to eat.

Green peppers. Cut pepper vertically down to the stem in 8 to 12 sections around the seed center. Break to eat.

Mushrooms. Trim stem ends. Eat small mushrooms whole. Cut large ones through cap only into 4 to 6 sections; break to eat.

Radishes. Cut off root ends and all but one or two leaves to hold for dipping.

Turnips. Peel and cut not quite through in thick slices. Break apart to eat.

Zucchini and yellow crookneck squash. Trim ends; cut not quite through in short sections. Break apart to eat.

Bagna Cauda Sauce

½ cup (¼ lb.) butter
¼ cup olive oil
4 small cloves garlic, mashed
1 can (2 oz.) anchovy fillets, well drained and finely chopped

Choose a heatproof container that will be only about half filled by the quantity of sauce you make. In it, combine butter, olive oil, and garlic. Add anchovy fillets and stir over moderate heat until mixture bubbles.

To serve, set over candle or low alcohol or canned heat flame. Mixture must not get hot enough to brown and burn. Makes 8 to 10 servings (or double recipe for 16 to 20 servings; triple it for 24 to 30 servings).

Mushrooms Bourguignonne

1 pound medium-sized
fresh mushrooms
1 cup Burgundy or Pinot Noir
1 tablespoon minced shallots or
green onions
1 tablespoon minced parsley
1 crushed clove garlic
¼ cup (⅛ lb.) butter
¼ teaspoon salt
Black pepper

Just as Bordelaise pertains to Bordeaux, Bourguignonne refers to the Burgundy region of France. It usually means the dish is cooked with red Burgundy wine.

This time mushrooms are cooked in the Burgundian manner, and are excellent as an appetizer, or as a garnish with roast beef or with basic hamburgers.

To serve them as an appetizer, you can prepare them in a chafing dish (or electric frying pan, if you wish) and hold over the bain-marie to keep them hot. For an accompaniment to a roast, start cooking them after the meat has been removed from the oven. By the time the mushrooms are ready, the meat will have set (10 to 15 minutes is recommended) and will be easier to carve.

Clean mushrooms, removing stems (save stems for soups and sauces). Put mushroom caps in chafing dish with wine, shallots, parsley, garlic, butter, salt, and a few grindings of black pepper. Cook for 6 or 7 minutes, or until mushrooms are tender. Discard garlic before serving.

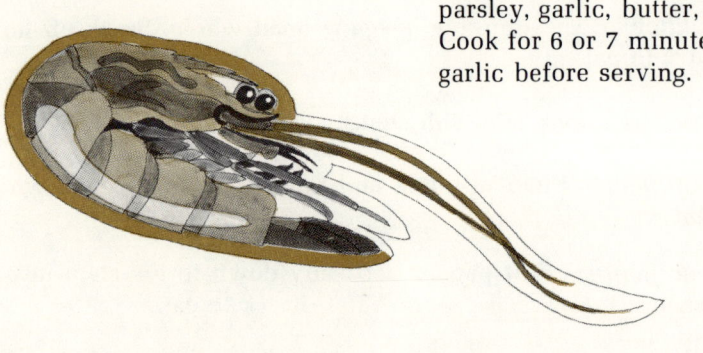

Sherried Shrimp with Tangy Sauce

1½ pounds raw shrimp or prawns,
peeled and deveined
¼ cup dry Sherry
4 tablespoons (⅛ lb.) butter
½ teaspoon garlic salt
¼ cup grated Parmesan cheese

Shrimp are marinated and cooked in Sherry, broiled briefly to a nice light brown, and then served directly from the chafing dish and dipped into a zippy sauce.

Place shrimp in a bowl and pour Sherry over them. Let marinate for several hours.

Melt butter in a frying pan over low heat. Add shrimp and Sherry. Sprinkle with garlic salt and simmer for 10 to 15 minutes. Just before serving, sprinkle cheese over shrimp, and place under broiler for 2 to 3 minutes, until cheese is lightly browned. Turn into a chafing dish or other container and keep warm over hot water or a candle. Makes appetizers for 6 to 8 people.

Tangy Sauce

½ cup mayonnaise
2 teaspoons lemon juice
1 tablespoon catsup
2 teaspoons Worcestershire
2 teaspoons prepared mustard

Thoroughly mix ingredients. Refrigerate until ready to use. Makes about ½ cup sauce.

Flaming Shrimp

2 pounds medium-sized shrimp
½ cup (¼ lb.) butter
Salt and pepper to taste
1 cup rum (80 proof)

Once the shrimp are deveined, this appetizer takes but 10 minutes more. Plan on flaming it at the buffet or coffee table.

In the kitchen: Shell and devein shrimp, leaving tails on. Sauté in butter until pink, about 5 minutes. Add salt and pepper.

At the table: heat rum in chafing dish. Add shrimp, and ignite rum. Shake pan, and spoon flaming rum over shrimp until flames burn down. Serve at once with cocktail forks or picks. Makes 8 appetizer servings.

Cherry Tomatoes and Shrimp in Herb Butter

½ cup (¼ lb.) butter
⅛ teaspoon curry powder
½ teaspoon basil, crumbled
¼ teaspoon celery seed
¼ teaspoon salt
Freshly ground pepper
1 pound medium-sized shrimp (about 40), shelled and deveined
1 cup firm ripe cherry tomatoes, stems removed
15 small tart shells (optional)

You simply simmer shrimp in an herb butter and add tomatoes to heat—and it's accomplished quite effortlessly, start to finish, right at the table.

Melt butter in chafing dish; add seasonings. When simmering, add shrimp and cook, stirring, until shellfish are bright pink (about 5 minutes).

Add tomatoes; heat, basting with butter, until heated through. Keep warm over low flame.

To serve, spear shrimp and tomato with cocktail picks, or spoon a few shrimp, a tomato, and some of the butter into a tart for each serving. Makes about 15 appetizers.

Dipping Kettle

2 slices meaty beef shanks, each 1 inch thick
4 chicken wings
1 slice ham hock, 1 inch thick (about ¼ pound)
3 carrots, cut in pieces
1 medium-sized onion, cut in pieces
1 bay leaf
5 or 6 whole black peppers
5 cups water
Salt to taste
About 1 pound loaf rye bread, cut in ¾-inch cubes, buttered and toasted
About 2 pounds thinly sliced boiled ham

The Swedish Christmas Eve custom of letting guests serve themselves from the dipping kettle adapts smoothly to the chafing dish. As the rich stock simmers away, each guest spears a chunk of toasted rye bread with a fork, dunks the bread in the stock, and then wraps it in a slice of ham to pop in his mouth.

Place shanks, chicken wings, ham hock, carrots, onion, bay leaf, and whole peppers in a large kettle. Add water and 1 teaspoon salt. Bring to a boil, cover, and simmer slowly for 4 hours.

Strain stock, discarding all fat, bones, skin (if desired), and bay leaf. Grind remaining meat and vegetables or whirl with some of the stock in a blender; return to stock. Adjust salt.

Pour stock into chafing dish; let simmer. Serve with rye bread cubes for dipping and with sliced ham cut in pieces just large enough to encircle bread. Makes appetizers for 16 people.

APPETIZERS ... USING TABLE TOP COOKWARE

Aïoli

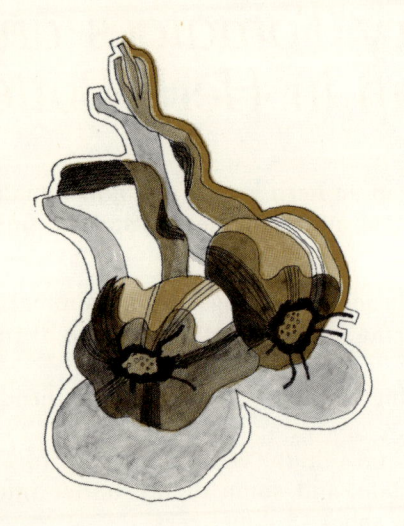

One sniff of golden aïoli (eye-o-lee) sauce and it becomes quite clear that garlic is its principal ingredient.

This lyrically-named mayonnaise is either an appetizer or an entire meal, the latter when the sauce is served with a variable collection of fish, shellfish, and vegetables—accompanied by nothing more than crusty bread.

The sauce is served cold, with an assortment of hot and cold foods. Use your chafing dish and other table top cooking and warming units to keep the hot foods at serving temperature.

Indications are that aïoli came from the early Greeks; they still have a similar, coarser aïoli sauce that involves bread crumbs pounded with garlic and oil, and sometimes walnuts or mashed potatoes.

The transfer of name as well as flavor to France probably occurred in the dim past when Greek colonists populated France's southern coast. Or it might have happened when the Romans, who prized Greek cooking and its civilized refinements, moved in later.

Since the meal remains typically peasant-style and help-yourself, you have great latitude in presenting the food. If you serve it from the center of a big roomy table, with knives and cutting boards handy to all, you can leave the cleaned foods whole and looking fresh from the garden, letting guests break or cut them up as they wish.

For buffet service, dishing up is simplified if the larger pieces are precut, then reassembled to preserve their appearance.

Aïoli—The Sauce

6 to 8 medium-sized or 4 large cloves garlic
1½ tablespoons lemon juice
½ teaspoon salt
3 egg yolks
½ cup salad oil
½ cup olive oil
Water

Put in a blender the garlic, lemon juice, salt, and egg yolks. Cover and whirl for about 1 minute or until the mixture is rather smooth. Continue to blend at high speed, adding in a slow steady stream the oils which have been mixed together. Add oil faster when mixture thickens, but never so quickly that it stands in puddles.

When the sauce becomes so thick that the oil is hard to incorporate (usually after you've added about half the oil), blend in 1 to 2 tablespoons water, then add remaining oil slowly. (If sauce ceases to take up oil, shut off blender, stir sauce and add a little oil or a little more water, and blend again; repeat as necessary.)

If you do not have a blender, force garlic through a garlic press and combine in a bowl with lemon juice, salt, and egg yolks. Beat with a rotary blender or wire whip until blended. Add oil a few drops at a time, beating rapidly and constantly. When sauce thickens, you can add more oil, but no faster than it can be easily mixed in. Thin with water if needed.

Chill sauce, covered, for at least several hours to mellow flavors; it keeps for about 4 days, after which the garlic flavor fades. Makes 1¾ cups, at least 6 generous servings.

APPETIZERS . . . USING TABLE TOP COOKWARE

Aïoli—The Meal

The array you present with the sauce can be freely chosen from available fish, shellfish, and vegetables—but no meat.

As mentioned, the meal being a help-yourself situation, it is best to make available a wide variety of fresh foods. Simply wash, arrange attractively uncut, or slice into serving pieces and put back together for attractive appearance.

The foods that aïoli complements include:

Hot boiled new potatoes (the only dish that really requires last-minute cooking).

Hot or cold cooked green beans and artichokes.

Cold cooked shrimp and lobster (in shells, but remove lobster meat, cut, and return to shell).

Hot or cold poached halibut, lingcod, or other lean white fish (served whole if possible).

Hard-cooked eggs.

Raw vegetables: fennel (also called sweet anise or finocchio), red or white cabbage (cut or to be cut in wedges), cherry tomatoes or regular tomatoes (to cut in wedges), mushrooms, turnips and zucchini (sliced partly through to snap apart), cauliflower, green peppers (seeded if desired), Belgian endive, and small inner romaine leaves.

Allow ⅓ to ½ pound completely edible fish or shellfish for each person. Figure the equivalent of one artichoke, green pepper, and turnip per person (a generous portion); then cut back this vegetable total about a third to a half in order to substitute small quantities of several other vegetables and give good variety.

Also allow about ¼ cup aïoli sauce per serving.

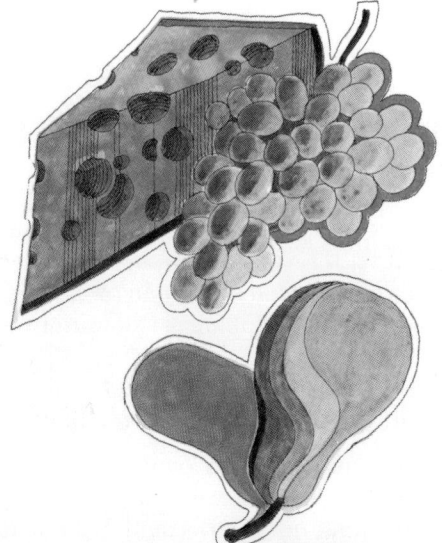

Pears and Apples with Smoked Cheese Dip

2 tablespoons butter
3 tablespoons flour
½ teaspoon dry mustard
2 cups milk or light cream
3 cups (¾ lb.) shredded hickory smoked process cheese
½ cup Sauterne
1 tablespoon cognac or brandy
Pears (Bartlett or Comice) and apples (Jonathan, Red or Yellow Delicious), about 4 of each
French bread chunks (optional)

Smoked cheese, Sauterne, and cream go together in this smooth, hot sauce to serve with wedges of juicy Bartlett pears and crisp apples. Prepared in a ceramic or heatproof container and kept warm over a candle, this dip is appropriate as an appetizer or fireside snack.

Melt butter in a pan and blend in flour and mustard; cook until bubbly. Gradually add milk, stirring, and cook until thickened.

Add cheese and stir over medium heat until melted. Blend in wine and cognac.

Place mixture over a small candle warmer (or on an electric trivet or warming tray) and dip cored wedges of pears and apples and chunks of bread into sauce. Stir sauce occasionally; thin, if necessary with warmed milk or light cream. Makes about 4 cups of sauce or 8 to 10 servings.

Appetizer Meatballs

¾ cup soy sauce
¾ cup water
2 small cloves garlic, mashed
2 teaspoons ground ginger
3 pounds ground chuck or round steak
Parsley for garnish
Toothpicks

Even though miniature meatballs take time to do, they're worth efforts expended because of their consistent appeal as party food. This recipe tastes like teriyaki steak. It makes approximately 175 appetizing morsels.

Prepare the meatballs in advance, but bake them just before serving. Serve from the chafing dish, utilizing the water bath to keep them piping hot but unscorched.

In a large bowl, combine the soy sauce, water, garlic, and ginger; mix until blended. Add the ground meat and blend lightly but thoroughly. Shape into balls the size of large marbles.

Arrange on shallow baking pans. Put into a 500° oven for 4 to 5 minutes, or until lightly browned; turn if needed to brown both sides.

Lift meatballs out of pans and into a chafing dish to keep hot for serving. Pour pan juices over meatballs. Garnish with parsley; serve with picks. Makes about 175 appetizer meatballs.

Appetizer Pancakes

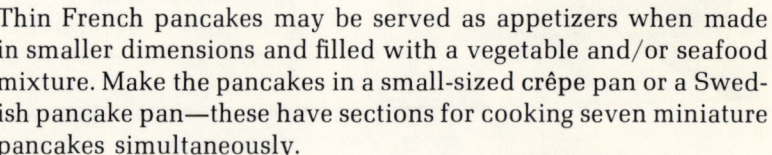

1 egg
1 cup milk
½ cup regular all-purpose flour (unsifted)
About 4 tablespoons butter or margarine
Filling (2 recipes follow)

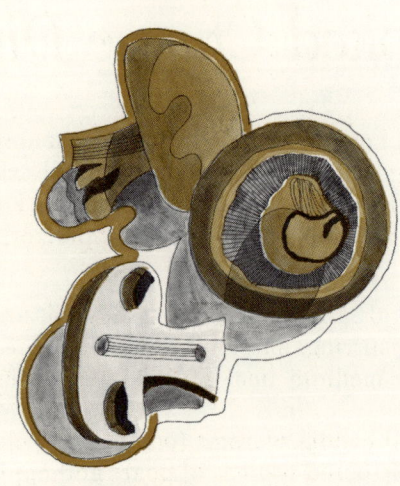

Thin French pancakes may be served as appetizers when made in smaller dimensions and filled with a vegetable and/or seafood mixture. Make the pancakes in a small-sized crêpe pan or a Swedish pancake pan—these have sections for cooking seven miniature pancakes simultaneously.

Your chafing dish with the water pan is the perfect place to keep them so they'll stay hot during the hors d'oeuvres hour.

Combine the egg, milk, and flour in a blender container. Blend 30 seconds, clean blender sides, then blend about 1 minute more. Or, combine the egg, milk, and flour in a bowl and beat with a rotary beater just until mixture is smooth, about 30 seconds. If rotary beater is used, let batter stand at room temperature for about 30 minutes after beating.

If you use a Swedish pancake pan, place over medium heat until hot enough to make a drop of water dance. Drop about ⅛ teaspoon butter into each indentation.

Using a measuring tablespoon, dip up about 2 teaspoons of the batter and pour into each indentation; quickly tip and tilt pan at each addition to distribute batter evenly. Pancakes will begin to set on top and brown underneath almost immediately. Turn with a small spatula and brown other sides; stack pancakes as they are removed from pan. Add butter to indentations each time. Makes about 40.

With a crêpe pan, make tiny pancakes one at a time, using about same amount of batter for each, lightly greasing pan for each pancake.

To fill pancakes, spread about 1 teaspoon filling down the middle of each and roll; arrange about half the pancakes, seam side down, in a buttered chafing dish; drizzle with 1 tablespoon melted butter. Cover and heat over simmering water until hot, about 15 minutes. Repeat with remaining rolls.

Each of these fillings makes enough for 1 recipe of pancakes, about 40.

Crab and Chive Filling

2 ounces (part of package) cream cheese
½ pound flaked crab meat
3 tablespoons whipping cream
1 tablespoon chopped chives or green onions

Soften cream cheese by stirring over hot water. Add crab meat, cream, and chives or green onion. Cook over boiling water until heated through, stirring to combine thoroughly.

Curried Mushroom Filling

4 teaspoons butter or margarine
4 teaspoons flour
⅛ teaspoon curry powder (or to taste)
¼ teaspoon salt
½ cup milk
2 tablespoons butter or margarine
½ pound fresh mushrooms, chopped
1 large onion, chopped

In a saucepan, melt 4 teaspoons butter over medium heat. Add flour, curry, and salt; heat, stirring, until bubbly.

Remove from heat and slowly stir in milk; continue stirring and heating until mixture boils. Remove from heat and set aside.

In a frying pan, melt 2 tablespoons butter over medium heat; add mushrooms and onion. Cook, stirring frequently, until onions are limp and mushroom juices have evaporated. Stir vegetables into sauce.

Spicy Meatballs

⅓ cup brown sugar, firmly packed
1 can (8 oz.) tomato sauce
3 tablespoons lemon juice
⅛ teaspoon garlic salt
½ cup dry red wine
About 1 small potato, peeled
1 pound ground chuck or lean ground beef
1 small onion, finely minced
1 egg
1 teaspoon salt

These bite-sized appetizers can be completely prepared a day ahead, then rewarmed before the party begins. A chafing dish keeps them hot during the festivities.

In a saucepan, combine the brown sugar, tomato sauce, lemon juice, garlic salt, and wine. Bring to a boil, stirring; reduce heat, and allow to simmer gently, uncovered, until sauce is thickened, about 20 minutes.

Finely shred enough potato to make ⅓ cup. Combine potato with meat, onion, egg, and salt until blended. Shape into balls the size of large marbles.

Arrange on shallow baking pans. Put into a 500° oven for 4 to 5 minutes, or until lightly browned. Remove and add to the prepared sauce, including any pan juices. Cool, then cover and refrigerate if made ahead.

To serve, heat meat and sauce together slowly. Makes about 5 dozen meatballs.

Note: Instead of wine, you could use ½ cup water plus 1 tablespoon lemon juice.

APPETIZERS... USING TABLE TOP COOKWARE

For a change of pace . . . shrimp, chunks of salmon, and tender scallops are being cooked in oil.

Fondue... with Cheese, Oil, Broth

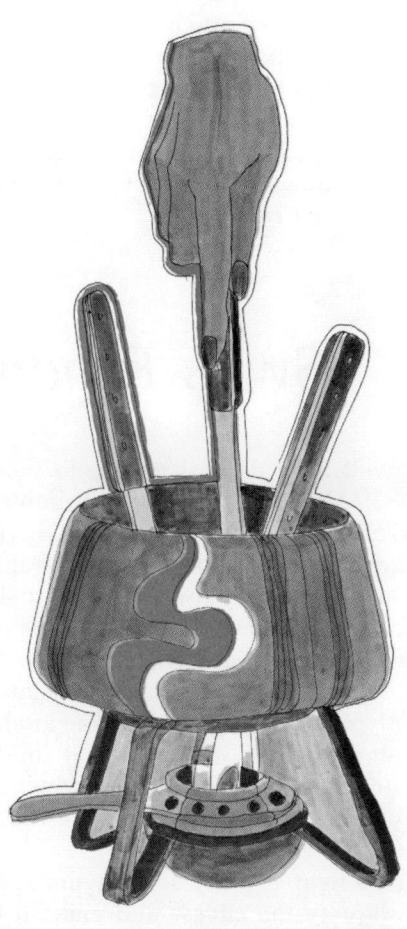

The word "fondue" is a derivation of the French word *fondre*, which means "to melt", but this only partially defines the word as it is used today.

The original fondue is thought to have been a Swiss dish, created to revive cheese and bread that became inedibly hard during the cold winter months. When shreddings of cheese were combined with a little warmed wine and chunks of bread dipped in the sauce, both cheese and bread became quite palatable.

Today the term "fondue" has a much broader meaning, referring to foods that are dunked, heated, or cooked in sauce, oil, or broth in a "fondue" (or similar) pot. Some units use denatured alcohol, others canned heat; some are convertible and can use either. In addition, there are a number of electric fondue pots which eliminate temperature guesswork since they are regulated for dessert, cheese, and oil or broth. Most are designed as all-purpose fondue pots with temperature controls that allow you to use them for cheese fondue and other low-temperature cooking.

Fondue Bourguignonne, for example, consists of cubes of tender meat that are cooked in hot oil. This fondue resembles the Oriental pots of broth in which meats and vegetables are cooked at the table.

This chapter will discuss the cheese fondues and those in which meat, fish, fowl, and vegetables are actually cooked in oil or broth. With each type of fondue, you'll find some helpful suggestions about the equipment and choosing and preparing the ingredients.

A selection of sauces or condiments usually accompany the fondues that cook in oil or broth. Recipes for fondue sauces are in the chapter beginning on page 37. The fondue desserts—usually a warm sauce for dipping morsels of fruit or uniced cake—are in the desserts chapter (see pages 66-79).

Fondue can also be a party appetizer. Some that are especially appropriate are included with other appetizers in the chapter beginning on page 11, but many of the recipes in this chapter can be served as appetizers.

FONDUE 23

Introduction to Cheese Fondue

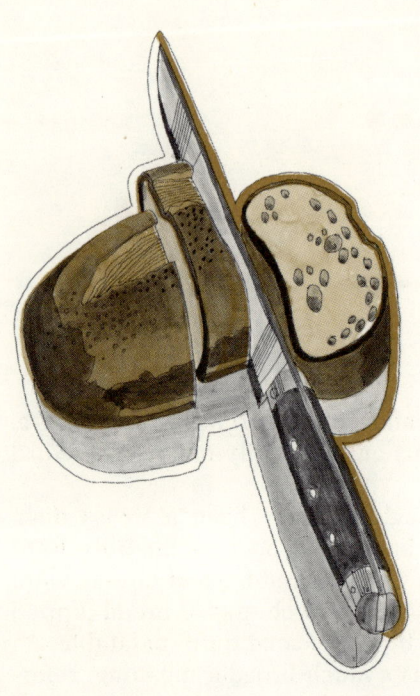

A pot of bubbling cheese fondue can provide an evening of good food and fun when you entertain a small group of people. You can serve cheese fondue to a larger group if you provide several small tables, each with its own pot of fondue.

Cheese fondue can also be a fine party appetizer, provided the guests understand that once the fondue is made, it must be stirred continuously to keep the sauce blended and smooth. This is easily accomplished if each guest gives the pot a good stir each time he dips in with a cube of bread.

The pots made especially for cheese fondue are of heavy, heat resistant earthenware or heavy metal which, when used over a controllable heat unit, maintain the low, even heat that is important for melting cheese into a smooth sauce. You can also use a casserole of heat resistant glass or ceramic material, a heavy metal pan, or a classic fondue bourguignonne pan (see page 5) over a well-regulated alcohol, canned heat, or butane flame, or over an electric hot plate or candle warmer. A chafing dish with the water pan or a double boiler may also be used. Follow the manufacturer's directions for using an electric fondue pot.

Your heat source should maintain a temperature that will keep the cheese at the simmering point, never much lower and definitely not any higher. If the cheese mixture gets too cool, it becomes tough; if the mixture becomes too hot, it gets stringy.

Our recipes begin with the classic Swiss fondue. It requires careful attention to details to insure its success, although none are difficult to master. We also include a selection of other cheese fondue recipes to extend your recipe repertoire.

Swiss Fondue

1 clove garlic, cut in half
2 cups light dry white wine (such as Riesling, Chablis, or Traminer)
½ pound imported Swiss cheese (Emmenthaler), shredded or cut in small dice
½ pound Swiss Gruyère or Danish Samsoe, shredded or cut in small dice
1 tablespoon cornstarch
1 teaspoon dry mustard (optional)
3 tablespoons kirsch (optional)
Freshly ground nutmeg and pepper, to taste
1 small loaf French bread, cut in bite-sized cubes with some crust on each

It is essential to use a very well aged natural cheese to insure success with this recipe classic. Most traditional and reliable is a combination of half Swiss Emmenthaler and half Swiss Gruyère or Danish Samsoe. Also recommended is a mixture of half Danish Tybo and half Samsoe. Or you can use only Swiss Emmenthaler.

It is also essential to have the correct heat for melting the cheese—hot enough to keep it bubbling slowly, but not so hot that it causes the cheese to separate. You can melt the cheese in an earthenware dish directly over a low heat on your kitchen range, or over simmering water if you're using a metal fondue pot. Once the cheese is melted, the fondue can be brought to the table and placed over your heating unit so the sauce keeps bubbling slowly.

In preparing cheese fondue, a light, slightly acetic wine is recommended. Acidity helps to liquefy the cheese and make it homogenous, and it also adds interesting flavor. Use a light dry white wine such as Riesling, Chablis, Traminer, Swiss Neuchâteloise, Rhine, or Moselle. If you don't feel your wine is sufficiently acetic, add a little lemon juice—about 1 teaspoon for each cup of wine.

As soon as the wine is warm and air bubbles are forming (never let the wine boil), the cheese is added by handfuls. Blend in thoroughly before introducing the next handful.

To keep the cheese from sticking to the bottom (some will adhere), have guests one at a time swirl their bread cubes around in a figure-8 motion. A quick little fillip on the way out of the pot prevents the cheese from dripping.

Should the fondue become too thick, add a small amount of *warmed, never cold,* wine and stir in completely.

Each bite-sized piece of bread—usually slightly dry French bread, although sour dough, rye, or other variety breads may be used—should be cut so there is one edge with crust. The bread cube goes on the fork from the soft edge, which means that the crust goes into the cheese first.

Halfway through the meal, it is traditional to offer small glasses of kirsch (cherry brandy), which is said to promote digestion and stimulate the appetite. After the fondue, you could serve a salad—either a green salad with oil and vinegar dressing or a light fruit salad—or just offer fruit for dessert.

On other occasions you may want to make just one pot of fondue to serve with beverages before dinner. The first recipe will provide appetizers for about a dozen guests.

If, somewhere along the way, the cube of bread should drop off into the fondue, the dunker has a choice of "traditional penalties". Men may either buy the next round of drinks, the next bottle of wine, or, if agreed upon, pay the entire bill if you're at a restaurant.

A woman who comes back with an empty fork has a choice of kissing her partner, the man beside her, or all the men participating in the communal dunking.

It might be wise to agree upon the "penalty" prior to getting the swirling underway.

By the time you reach the bottom, there is a crusty layer of cheese, a choice delicacy reserved either for the guest of honor, if there is one, or perhaps for the person who kept his bread on the fork throughout the dunking.

Rub sides and bottom of the fondue pot with the cut garlic. Add wine; heat slowly until bubbles form and slowly rise to the surface. Combine the two cheeses, cornstarch, and mustard (if used). Add cheese mixture, a spoonful at a time; stir slowly and continuously until all the cheese is blended into a smooth sauce—it should bubble very slowly. (The Swiss insist it should be stirred in a figure-8 pattern with a wooden fork.)

Stir in kirsch (if used) a tablespoon at a time, and again bring to a slow boil. (If the heat gets too high at any time, the fondue may separate.) Sprinkle with nutmeg and pepper to taste. Take to the table, along with bread cubes, and adjust heat so fondue keeps bubbling *slowly*. Guests swirl bread cubes in a figure-8 pattern through cheese.

If the fondue should get too thick, thin with a little heated wine. Makes 4 servings as entree or 12 servings as an appetizer.

Swiss Cheese Dipping Sauce

1½ to 1¾ cups half-and-half (half milk, half cream), or half white wine or beer with half-and-half
1 pound process Swiss cheese, diced or shredded
3 tablespoons flour
½ teaspoon dry mustard
Pinch of nutmeg
Seasoned salt to taste
French bread cubes or other dippers

Flavor depends entirely upon the choice of liquid selected to thin the cheese. Half-and-half or half-and-half accented with wine or beer may be used.

Process cheese is usually reliable and rarely becomes tough or stringy. However, it tends to thicken more readily than natural cheese and normally needs to be thinned if it stands very long.

This is a flexible recipe that can be used for a variety of occasions. For brunch you might serve it with cubes of ham and toast to dip into the pot of melted cheese.

Heat 1½ cups liquid(s) to just below boiling point. Combine cheese, flour, mustard, nutmeg, and seasoned salt. Add to hot liquid by handfuls and stir briskly until thickened and well blended. Place over low flame to keep cheese simmering but not boiling, adding more of the warmed half-and-half or other liquid as needed to keep a good dipping consistency. Serves 5 or 6 as part of entree or as appetizer.

Buttermilk Cheese Dipping Sauce

Follow the recipe for Swiss Cheese Dipping Sauce, substituting 1½ to 1¾ cups buttermilk for the half-and-half and other liquids. You might also omit mustard and nutmeg; flavor it instead with 1 clove garlic, halved, and heated with the buttermilk, then removed, and ⅛ teaspoon pepper.

This makes an interesting brunch dish when served with asparagus spears that have been cooked just until tender, then chilled; bockwurst sausages (pour boiling water over sausages, cover, and let stand 20 minutes, then drain, cool, and remove casings, and cut into ¾-inch-thick slices); cherry tomatoes; and rye bread slices. At the table, dip the vegetables and sausages in cheese and use the bread to catch drips en route from pot to plate.

Brunch Swiss Fondue

½ pound shredded process Swiss cheese (2 cups)
1½ tablespoons cornstarch
¼ teaspoon salt
⅛ teaspoon dry mustard
⅛ teaspoon nutmeg
⅛ teaspoon pepper
1 cup buttermilk
1 clove garlic
Dry white table wine
Ham cubes
Toast croutons

Serve this version with ham cubes and toast croutons for swirling. To complete the menu: Chilled fresh fruits or a curried compote, heated Danish pastries, and, if desired, a scrambled egg dish.

Toss cheese with cornstarch, salt, dry mustard, nutmeg, and pepper. Heat buttermilk with garlic over hot water in fondue pot or chafing dish. When hot, remove garlic and add cheese mixture. Stir until cheese melts and blends smoothly.

Add heated wine gradually, about 2 tablespoons at a time, to keep fondue at dipping consistency. Serve with ham cubes and toast croutons.

Fonduta

8 ounces Fontina or Fontinella cheese, shredded (or 6 oz. Mozzarella and 2 oz. Bel Paese cheeses)
½ cup half-and-half (half milk, half cream)
1 teaspoon flour
Dash white pepper
3 egg yolks, slightly beaten
1 can (1 oz.) white truffles (optional)
2 or 4 tablespoons half-and-half
1 tablespoon butter
French bread cubes or bread sticks

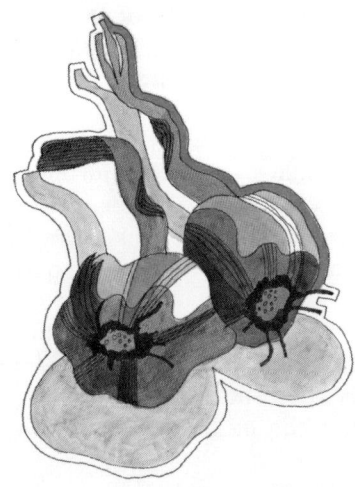

The Italian version of cheese fondue differs from the Swiss recipe in several ways. First, the Swiss idea is basically cheese and wine; fonduta is essentially an egg custard with cheese added for flavor and thickening.

Both the Fontina cheese and the distinctive white truffles that perfume this fondue come from the Piedmont region of northern Italy. Although the cheese may be found in most cheese stores and delicatessens, the truffles will require a trip to a well-stocked specialty food establishment.

Results are still interesting even if truffles are omitted, and similar flavor is obtained by using an alternate to the more expensive Fontina or Fontinella—the combination of mild Mozzarella and light and creamy Bel Paese.

For best results, prepare the fonduta first in a double boiler, then transfer to a chafing dish with warm water in the bain-marie.

Place cheese in shallow bowl; stir in the ½ cup half-and-half. Cover and let stand for 30 minutes.

Meanwhile, blend flour and pepper with egg yolks. Drain 2 tablespoons of the liquid from the truffles, if used; add the 2 tablespoons half-and-half (if truffles are omitted, use the 4 tablespoons half-and-half).

Blend liquid into egg yolk mixture. Slice truffles paper thin with a vegetable peeler or very sharp knife. Blend egg yolk mixture into cheese.

Cook over gently boiling water (water should not touch underside of upper portion of the double boiler), stirring constantly, until cheese melts and mixture is just thickened and smooth. Stir in butter until melted.

Place in chafing dish over warm water to serve. Eat, fondue style, with bread cubes on fondue forks or bamboo skewers, or use bread sticks to dip up mixture. Makes 6 servings.

Shrimp Fondue

¾ pound large raw shrimp
Boiling salted water
2 tablespoons butter or margarine
2 tablespoons flour
¼ teaspoon salt
1¼ cups half-and-half (half milk, half cream)
1 tablespoon dry Sherry
½ cup grated Romano cheese
⅛ teaspoon paprika
Dash cayenne
French or sourdough bread
Carrot, cucumber, zucchini, and celery rounds or sticks

Shrimp Fondue may be prepared in either a chafing dish or ceramic fondue pot. Large shrimp are eaten from fondue fork or bamboo skewer; dip up the cheese sauce with small slices of sourdough bread or crisp raw vegetables.

Cook shrimp in boiling salted water to cover, just until shrimp turn pink; shell and devein.

Melt butter over direct heat in blazer pan of chafing dish or in fondue pot. Stir in flour and salt; cook until bubbly. Gradually add half-and-half and cook, stirring until thickened and smooth.

Blend in Sherry, cheese, paprika, and cayenne. Stir in shrimp.

Use bread, cut into two or three-bite size, and vegetable sticks and rounds to dip up sauce. Serves 4 to 6 as an appetizer, or 2 as entree.

Introduction to Oil Fondue

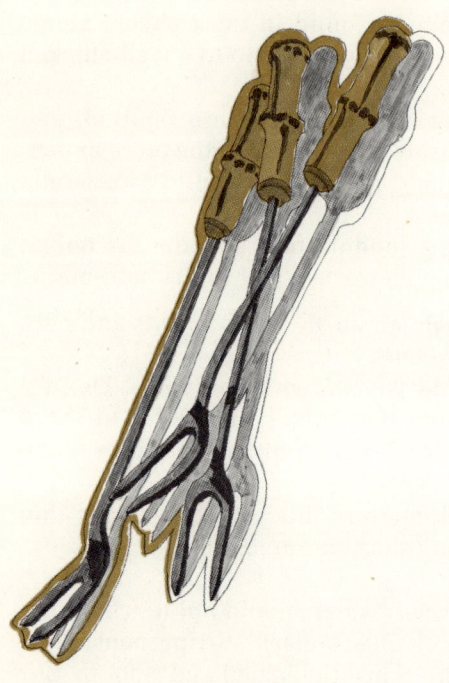

Oil fondues are an easy way to entertain, because everything can be done beforehand, and friends cook their own food.

Beef, lamb, chicken, fish, and seafood may be selected. All work beautifully and are ideal as appetizer, entree, mid- or late-evening meal.

A good cooking unit, one that keeps the pot of oil hot and that is safe to use at the table, is essential. There are a wide variety of oil fondue units on the market. Some are complete sets, including burner, stand, metal pot, and a tray to protect the table and catch spatters.

You may choose between stainless steel, aluminum, porcelain or enamel-coated cast iron, copper, and silver plate or sterling silver. Non-stick coatings make cleaning easier.

The traditional fondue bourguignonne pan is wider at the base and curves in at the top. This eliminates some of the spattering and helps hold the heat. Most are 1½ to 2-quart capacity.

You can improvise the equipment for oil fondue cooking with any good heating unit that burns denatured alcohol, canned heat, or butane. The container for the oil can be an attractive saucepan. Choose one that is at least 3½ inches deep and not more than about 8 inches in diameter. One with straight sides or sides that curve inward at the top minimize splattering. Make sure the pan rests securely on the heat stand so that there is no danger of tipping.

Prices of fondue units vary from quite inexpensive to costly. Sturdiness of construction is the most important consideration; you should also be able to adjust the heat source if you're looking for an all-purpose container that can be used for more than oil cooking.

Forks and plates specifically designed for cooking and serving fondue are available in a variety of materials, shapes, sizes, colors, and price ranges.

Long bamboo skewers may be used, but metal fondue forks with insulated handles are more satisfactory, particularly with oil or broth fondues. Many manufacturers now include forks as part of their fondue sets and, most often, have color-keyed either handles or tips to make it easy for each person to keep track of his own utensil.

Two- and three-tined fork designs are available, and it doesn't seem to matter which one you select; most work equally well for bread or meat. They should be a minimum of 10 inches long, however, and tines should be generous in length and of sturdy material.

Plates with special sections—usually 4 or 5 small indentations for sauces and a large section for meat—are nice to have, but certainly not mandatory. They are available in china, pottery, plastic, or metal. Small bowls are used by many hostesses. These are passed around the table and guests choose their favorite sauces.

If you are serving fondue for the first time, it is a good idea to test your equipment well ahead of party time. Add salad oil to the pot as directed by the manufacturer of your unit—or not more than half full, if your unit has no book of directions. The amount of oil needed will vary with the size of your pot. It will be helpful to know how long it takes your unit to heat the oil to about 375°, the best temperature for cooking most meats. Use a deep fat frying thermometer to determine temperature or test with a piece of meat or with a cube of bread (the oil should sizzle upon contact with the meat and the meat should begin to brown immediately; the bread cube will brown in about 60 seconds).

Unless you have an electric fondue pot, it is best to heat the pot of oil on your range first, returning the pot to your kitchen range from time to time during the party, if necessary, to maintain the right cooking temperature. If the oil isn't hot enough, the meat will absorb too much oil and will not brown and cook quickly.

You will also want to prevent the oil from getting too hot. At about 440°, vegetable oils begin to smoke and discolor, which will adversely flavor the food. Learn how to regulate your unit when you need to reduce the heat. For some fondue recipes a combination of half clarified butter and half salad oil is preferred for flavor. This combination may be used with any of the following fondues, especially if buttery sauces are not served. Because butter breaks down and begins to smoke at a lower temperature than salad oil—about 405°—greater care is required to prevent overheating. It is important that the butter be clarified before it is combined with the oil to remove any milky sediment that would burn easily.

To clarify butter, put the required amount of butter (usually ½ to ¾ pound) in a deep saucepan or the top of a double boiler. Place over low heat and melt slowly, without stirring. Remove from heat and carefully skim off any foam. Slowly pour the clear yellow liquid from the top of the pan into another container, leaving the milky residue in the bottom of the pan. Cover and refrigerate, if made ahead. One pound of butter yields about 1½ cups of clarified butter.

Here are other pointers for cooking and serving oil fondue:

First, a good cut of meat is essential. With beef, sirloin or tenderloin are recommended; leg is suggested for lamb; preferred seafoods include shrimp, scallops, and salmon. Allow about ⅓ to ½ pound per serving as the main course; from ⅛ to ¼ pound as appetizer, depending upon other foods. The meat should be well trimmed of fat and gristle, then cut into bite-sized cubes. Fish should, of course, be completely free of bones or shell.

All foods should be dried off, or not noticeably juicy, to decrease spattering during cooking.

To facilitate cooking, remove the meat or fish from the refrigerator about 15 to 30 minutes before serving so it will be nearly room temperature. This will keep the oil temperature higher, too, particularly important with an alcohol or canned heat burner.

In selecting the sauces to accompany fondue, it is best to serve a variety, usually between three and five—although you can serve more, or even just one. If you have special fondue plates with sections for sauces, the number you offer may be predetermined.

Oil fondue con't

Sauce suggestions begin on page 37. Almost all are easy to make and most benefit by being stirred up the evening or morning before the party to allow flavors to blend, if this is convenient.

Set the fondue scene by turning lights low, perhaps using candles for atmosphere. Cooking and eating can take place around the dining table, or, for added informality, set up the fondue on the coffee table and seat your guests on cushions around it.

Regardless of where the cooking takes place, protect the table with a washable mat or cloth. The trays that do come with some fondue sets help catch spatters, but often the oil pops beyond the tray.

Bright napkins and place mats in matching or contrasting colors are the only decorative requirements.

A final caution that merits repeating: Provide each person with a fork for removing the meat from the fondue fork. This isn't entirely for sanitary reasons, but to prevent burned lips if the mouth does happen to touch the boiled-in-oil metal fondue fork. (Additional safety precautions are mentioned on page 9.)

Remember, too, that meat and poultry fondues may be combined and cooked in the same oil simultaneously, but seafood fondue requires its own pot.

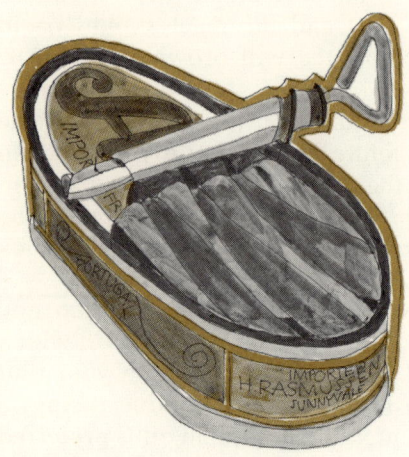

Fondue Bourguignonne

About 2 cups salad oil or about 1 cup each salad oil and clarified butter (see page 29)
2 to 2½ pounds boneless beef sirloin or tenderloin, well trimmed and cut in bite-sized cubes
Salt and pepper

To accompany this fondue, serve three to five sauces, selected from those in the Sauce chapter that begins on page 37. Béarnaise and Hollandaise sauces are old favorites. For good contrast in flavor and appearance, you might also serve a teriyaki-flavored sauce, a tangy sour-cream-based sauce, a barbecue or other tomato-based sauce, and a sweet-and-sour or chutney sauce.

The only other accompaniments needed to round out a meal of Beef Bourguignonne are a crisp green salad, crusty sour dough bread, and a dry red wine. You might also include fresh mushrooms (about ¾ pound to serve 4), sliced lengthwise in halves or quarters. They can be eaten raw or cooked in the oil.

In fondue pot heat oil over low range temperature to about 375° or use electric fondue pot as manufacturer directs. Oil should be hot enough so that meat sizzles and browns quickly as it touches the oil.

When oil is ready, carefully bring to the table and place over heating unit. Let each guest cook his own fondue as follows: Spear a cube of meat with fork or skewer and hold it in the oil until meat is cooked as desired. Allow about 30 seconds for medium rare, although this varies slightly depending upon the temperature of the meat and oil and the size of the cube. Transfer the meat to the dinner plate with another fork, and use the fondue fork to start another meat cube cooking. Season the cooked meat with salt and pepper and dip into sauces, as desired. Makes 4 servings.

30   FONDUE . . . OIL

Lamb Fondue

1 leg of lamb (about 5 pounds), boned
About 2 cups salad oil or half salad oil and half clarified butter (see page 29)
Tomato Lemon Chutney
Chutney

Cubes of lamb cooked in oil (or part butter-part oil) are served here with a selection of sauces. Chutney combinations on pages 42-43 are recommended accompaniments.

You might also serve a flavored rice as a side dish, and a crisp bread such as toasted flour tortillas.

Have your meatman bone leg of lamb. Trim off and discard fat and connective tissue; then cut meat in bite-sized cubes (this process takes time, but you can do it a day ahead). Cover and chill the meat until about 30 minutes before ready to serve.

Fill fondue pot ⅓ to ½ full with oil; heat to about 375°, or use electric fondue pot as manufacturer directs. Oil should be hot enough so that meat sizzles and browns quickly as it touches the oil. Place over table top heating element; adjust heat to keep oil at correct temperature.

Let guests spear 2 or 3 pieces at a time on bamboo skewers or fondue forks and immerse meat in hot fat to cook until done as desired.

With a fork, push meat from skewers onto individual plates, or on top of rice if it is served as an accompaniment. Pass chutney sauces to spoon onto plate. Makes 4 to 6 servings.

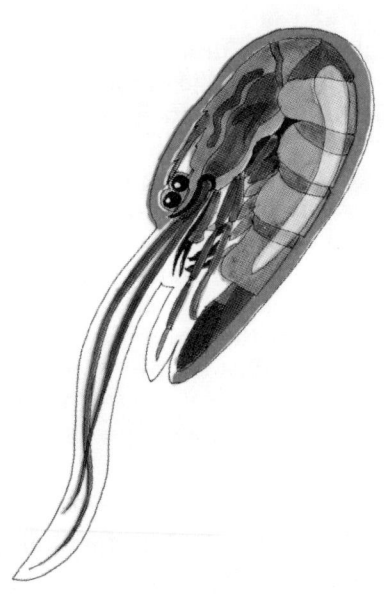

Seafood Fondue

½ pound salmon steaks
½ pound swordfish steaks
¾ pound medium-sized raw shrimp
½ pound scallops
About 2 cups salad oil or half salad oil and half clarified butter (see page 29)

Friends who like seafood should enjoy selecting from scallops, salmon, swordfish, and shrimp. Bottled or homemade seafood cocktail sauce, a chutney sauce, and guacamole or avocado sauces are good complements. You might also offer wedges of lemon. Caesar Salad, sourdough bread or rolls, and a fruit and cheese dessert could round out this meal.

Cut salmon and swordfish into ¾-inch squares, discarding skin and bones. Peel and devein shrimp. Cut scallops into bite-sized pieces. Arrange in separate sections on a bed of lettuce or other greens.

Fill fondue pot ⅓ to ½ full with oil; heat to about 375°, or use electric fondue pot as manufacturer directs. Oil should be hot enough so that fish sizzles and oil bubbles rather vigorously immediately upon contact. Place over table top heating element; adjust heat to keep oil at correct temperature.

Arrange tray of fish and condiment sauces alongside the fondue pot.

Let each person spear a piece of fish with a fondue fork or bamboo skewer and dip it into the bubbling oil to cook. When fish takes on a tinge of brown on its edges (this takes about a minute depending upon temperature of fish and oil and size of pieces), it is usually done. Makes 4 servings.

Seafood-Vegetable Tempura

Uncooked fish and shellfish (select from following allowing ¾ pound per person): Crab, shelled, in chunks; Fish, boneless and cut in bite-sized pieces; Lobster tails, shelled and sliced across the grain; Oysters and clams, drained and cut in half; Scallops, cut in half; Shrimp, shelled (leave tails on), deveined, split almost through vein side, spread flat, scored lightly with cross-hatch pattern

Vegetables (select from following allowing ½ to ¾ pound, total, per person): Asparagus, cut in 1-inch diagonal slices; Carrots and celery, cut in thin, diagonal slices; Eggplant, cut in ¼-inch slices and quartered; Green beans, boiled 5 minutes, drained, cut in 2-inch lengths; Green onions, cut in 1 to 2-inch lengths; Fresh mushrooms, sliced or whole if small; Spinach, small leaves with all but ½ inch of stem removed; Summer squash, cut in ½-inch slices; Sweet potatoes, peeled and thinly sliced; Watercress, broken in small branches

Batter (recipe follows)
About 2 cups salad oil
Tempura sauce (see page 45)
Lemon wedges with salt

This Japanese tempura uses an assortment of seafoods and vegetables which are batter-coated and fried in oil until crisp. The batter recipe is enough to coat foods for a main dish serving 4 to 6 people, or for appetizers serving about 12 people.

Electric fondue pot, tempura pan or deeper frying pan, or alcohol, butane, or canned-heat-fueled fondue bourguignonne pot may be used for cooking. Perhaps more dramatic and very convenient, too, is a *Tempura nabe*—a special pan with a rack on the side for draining. This may be used over an electric hot plate that has several heat settings, or, if you cook outdoors, the pan can be used over a hibachi that has good draft control.

Tempura requires a slightly different cooking procedure from other oil fondues. Each food must first be dipped in the batter, then is drained briefly after frying. This procedure is easiest if the hostess dips the foods into the batter, adding enough foods to the oil so each guest receives several morsels each time. Foods are removed with a little wire skimmer or slotted spoon and allowed to drain on the rack (if a special tempura pan is used) or on a plate or basket covered with paper towels.

Guests then spear the fried foods with fondue forks or pick them up with chopsticks. Serve tempura simply with lemon wedges and salt, or with the special tempura sauce. You might also offer grated fresh ginger and grated Japanese *daikon* (a giant white radish), which is added to each guest's sauce as desired.

Hot steamed rice is the usual accompaniment.

Have ready a cake rack on a shallow pan or tray for draining the pieces (unless you have a *Tempura nabe*).

Fill fondue pot ⅓ to ½ full with oil; heat to about 375°, or use electric fondue pot as manufacturer directs.

Dip the prepared food into the batter, holding it by tail or stem, or with chopsticks or tongs. Let it drip a second, then put into the hot oil. Cook until golden brown.

It is wise to turn the foods a few seconds after they are put into the fat; this makes subsequent turning easier. Remove fried foods with a second set of chopsticks, tongs, slotted spoon, or wire skimmer. Skim out any drops of batter so they won't burn.

Do not cook too much food at one time or it will cool the oil too fast. If the temperature drops below 350°, the food will absorb oil and not be crisp. Put in first the foods that must cook longer, such as shrimp; add those like spinach last (as a general rule, you may cook 4 or 5 pieces at a time in an electric vessel; 2 or 3 over an alcohol or canned heat burner).

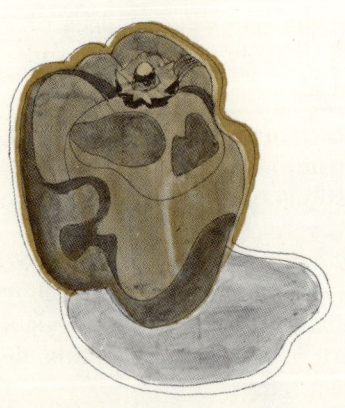

Batter

2 eggs
15 tablespoons (1 cup minus 1 tablespoon) cold water
¾ cup unsifted flour
½ teaspoon salt (optional)

Combine eggs with water; beat until frothy. Beat in flour and salt until blended—don't beat the flour any more than is necessary. Set the bowl of batter inside another bowl with ice, to keep it cold.

32 FONDUE... OIL

Introduction to Broth Fondue

Another kind of fondue is that in which meats or fish and vegetables are cooked in broth. The foods poach in the liquid rather than sear and brown as they do when cooked in oil. Besides the flavor given by a nicely seasoned broth, calories are lower.

As an extra bonus, the flavorful broth can be ladled into cups or bowls after the meats and vegetables have been cooked and served as a delicious light course following the fondue.

Broth may be substituted for salad oil to cook beef, lamb, chicken, fish, or shellfish. The ingredients are prepared and cooked in much the same way as for oil fondue.

A large metal fondue pot, any chafing-dish-type cooker that burns denatured alcohol or canned heat, an electric frying pan, or other electric cooker may be used. Or you can use the Oriental hot pot described in the recipe for Mizutaki. You need enough heat (and depth) to keep 2 to 3 inches of broth boiling.

Poached Seafood and Vegetables

¾ pound scallops, halved if large
½ pound medium-sized raw shrimp, deveined and shelled
1 pound salmon or swordfish, cut in bite-sized pieces
3 carrots, cut in bite-sized pieces
3 turnips, cut in bite-sized pieces
3 stalks celery, cut in ½-inch lengths
¼ pound fresh spinach
Lemon Mayonnaise Sauce (recipe on page 40)
2 cans (about 14 oz. each) regular-strength chicken broth
1 bottle (8 oz.) clam juice
1 clove garlic, mashed
About 3 cups hot, cooked rice

Two courses are cooked in the same pot for this meal. First the seafood is cooked in a seasoned broth to eat with rice and a special Lemon Mayonnaise Sauce. When the main course is completed, fresh spinach goes into the broth to make the soup.

Set the table for this meal with a plate, regular fork and spoon, and fondue fork or skewer at each place. Serve the mayonnaise sauce in Oriental soup bowls (about 1-cup size) or teacups that can be used later for soup. Serve the rice on the plate or in another small bowl.

Ahead of time, arrange scallops, shrimp, and salmon or swordfish on a serving plate. Cut and arrange carrots, turnips, and celery on a plate. Wash spinach for the soup; remove coarse stems and arrange in a bowl or basket. Prepare Lemon Mayonnaise Sauce. Cover and refrigerate until about 30 minutes before serving.

Shortly before serving time, combine chicken broth and clam juice in a pan; heat to boiling in the kitchen. Pour about half the broth into your fondue pot; keep the rest hot on the range.

Add carrots, turnips, celery and garlic to broth in fondue pot; heat to boiling, then bring to table; keep boiling.

At the table, add about half of each kind of shellfish and fish. As soon as fish is done (3 to 5 minutes), reduce heat.

Guests can begin spearing pieces of fish and vegetables from the pot and dipping them in the sauce, to eat with the rice, if desired. When most of the seafood has been eaten, replenish the pot with more broth, if needed, and cook remaining seafood.

Bring the spinach to the table after most of the seafood and vegetables have been eaten. Add remaining broth to the pot, then add the spinach. Stir and simmer about 1 minute. Ladle into sauce bowls to be stirred into remaining sauce. Makes 6 servings.

Mizutaki

BROTH
For 4 to 6 servings: 4 cans (14 oz. each) regular-strength beef or chicken broth; Water, enough to make 2 cups cooking liquid

MEATS
Select one kind or a variety from the following, allowing about ½ pound boneless meat per person: Beef sirloin, or any lean, tender beefsteak (flank, market, top round), cut 1½ to 2 inches thick across the grain; Chicken breasts or thighs, skinned, boned, and cut in 1-inch pieces; Pork or lamb, cut 1½ to 2 inches thick

VEGETABLES
Select several from the following: Carrots, peeled and thinly sliced; Cauliflower, cut into small flowerettes; Green onions or leeks, cut in 2-inch pieces; Fresh mushrooms, sliced; Fresh spinach (tender small leaves); Japanese tofu (soy bean curd), cubed; Japanese dried forest mushrooms, soaked until soft, with stems removed; Fresh asparagus spears; Broccoli flowerettes; Whole Chinese pod peas; Chinese cabbage, shredded; Watercress sprigs; Bamboo shoots, sliced; Water chestnuts, sliced; Green pepper strips

An important addition to the succulence of this Japanese dish is the rich and subtly seasoned sauce into which the cooked foods are dipped.

The classic pot for cooking Mizutaki is a charcoal-fired, metal pot with a center chimney, surrounded by a moat that holds the broth for cooking. These "hot pots" are widely available in import shops. When you use one, make sure your table is well protected from the intense heat of the charcoal.

There's a wide choice of ingredients for this recipe. Plan on about ½ pound boneless meat per person—it might be all one kind or several kinds. Then choose a variety of vegetables that will be compatible in flavors and offer pleasing color and texture contrasts.

The large variety of vegetables and meats call for a cooking procedure that differs from the each-morsel-on-a-fork technique used for most other fondues. Host or hostess fills the pot with a variety of the foods being offered, starting with the ingredients that take the longest to cook. Then after a few minutes of covered cooking, guests begin to remove the foods from the pot, using chopsticks or the special little wire baskets designed for this dish (available in Oriental stores). This process is repeated until the cooking is finished.

The meats and vegetables should be prepared ahead, arranged attractively on trays, covered with damp paper towels and refrigerated. You may also prepare the sauce ahead. Plan to have hot cooked rice ready when it is time to serve.

After all the foods are cooked, some of the broth is ladled into each guest's sauce bowl, blended with any remaining mizutaki sauce, and sipped.

Plan to serve hot tea throughout the meal. Dessert may be quite simple, such as fresh fruit or fruit sherbet, served with little rice cookies.

The procedure. At each place provide a bowl of the mizutaki sauce, a small plate, chopsticks, fork or wire basket, and a teacup.

Just before the diners are seated, bring the broth to boiling on the kitchen range and then pour enough into the cooking pot to fill it 2 to 3 inches deep; keep the rest of the broth simmering to replenish the pot during second and third cooking.

While still in the kitchen, you might put into the pot a selection of the items needing longest cooking (such as chicken, carrots, cauliflower, green onions, leeks), keeping each kind together in a separate area of the broth as much as possible. Cover and simmer about 5 minutes.

After guests are seated, bring the cooking pot to the table. Then add other ingredients. After 2 or 3 minutes more of cooking (with the cover on), guests begin to help themselves to a selection of the cooked foods, transferring them from the pot to the sauce bowl, rice bowl, or plate.

Fill the cooker again while the first servings are being eaten.

For a more leisurely meal, you could furnish each person with cooking chopsticks or the little wire ladles and let each do his own cooking.

Toward the end of dinner, ladle some of the cooking broth into each person's sauce bowl to be stirred into the sauce left in the bowl; sip like a soup.

Mizutaki Sauce

1 egg
2 tablespoons rice wine vinegar or other white wine vinegar
¼ teaspoon dry mustard
1 cup salad oil
⅓ cup sour cream
2 tablespoons soy sauce
2 tablespoons Mirin (rice wine) or Sherry
⅓ cup beef broth, chicken broth, or soup stock

This sauce starts with homemade mayonnaise, made in a blender; for a short cut, you may omit the eggs, vinegar, mustard, and oil and use instead 1¼ cups bottled mayonnaise. If sesame oil is available, add 1 teaspoon with the salad oil or mayonnaise.

In a blender, combine the egg, vinegar, dry mustard, and ¼ cup of the oil; whirl until blended. With blender motor on high, gradually add remaining oil in a slow steady stream. Whirl about 30 seconds more, then pour into a bowl. Stir in sour cream, soy, Mirin or Sherry, and broth. Refrigerate until serving time. Makes 1¼ cups, enough for 6 servings.

Chicken-Mushroom Fondue

About 3 pounds chicken breasts, boned and skinned
4 cans (about 14 oz. each) chicken broth
1 small bay leaf
5 whole cloves
2 teaspoons salt
¼ teaspoon basil leaves, crushed
¼ teaspoon white pepper
¾ cup dry white table wine
1 pound medium-sized fresh mushrooms, sliced

Lightly seasoned broth is used for cooking strips of chicken breast and slices of mushroom. Results are lower in calories—and cost—than the oil version. If you wish, make your own broth base using remaining meat and bones from breasts, adding a few necks and backs if it seems skimpy. Have enough broth on hand to replace that which is absorbed or evaporated in cooking. Excellent with Teriyaki Sauce (page 44), toasted sesame seeds, and Curry Dip (page 45). The curry sauce makes a delicious dip for the raw mushrooms while chunks of chicken are cooking.

For easy slicing, arrange boned chicken breasts in single layer on flat baking pan. Place in freezer about ½ hour or until surface is just slightly frozen. Remove from freezer and slice chicken in lengthwise strips (about ¼-inch wide and 3 inches long). Roll strips for easier skewering.

In the kitchen, simmer broth with bay leaf, cloves, salt, basil, and white pepper for about 15 minutes. Strain broth and add wine. Pour about half of the broth into your fondue pot and bring to boiling, then bring to table. Keep remaining broth hot in the kitchen.

To cook, spear a rolled chicken strip and a mushroom on fondue fork; place in boiling broth and cook about 2 to 3 minutes, or just until chicken is cooked through (meat turns white and becomes slightly fibrous). Replenish the broth as needed during the cooking. Makes 4 to 6 servings.

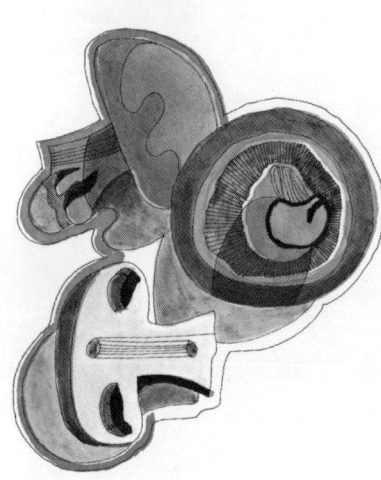

An assortment of sauces—sweet, spicy, mild, and tart—usually accompanies oil or broth fondues.

SAUCES FOR FONDUE

Sauces...Savory Accents to Complement Fondue

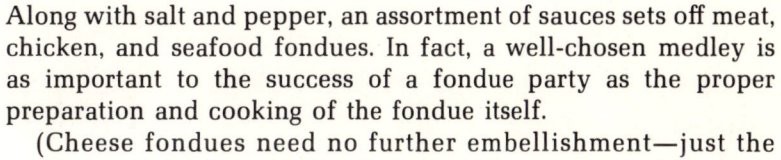

Along with salt and pepper, an assortment of sauces sets off meat, chicken, and seafood fondues. In fact, a well-chosen medley is as important to the success of a fondue party as the proper preparation and cooking of the fondue itself.

(Cheese fondues need no further embellishment—just the bread for dunking. In this book the specific sauces used for some chafing dish entrees appear with the recipes; and dessert sauces may be found in the desserts chapter.)

A combination of three to six sauces is most often served, although you and your friends may find you prefer a certain one above all others—or you could go the other way and whip up a dozen different mixtures.

Usually you will vary the array by including a sweet, a spicy, a mild, and a tart sauce.

Traditional favorites include Béarnaise, Hollandaise, horseradish, well-seasoned red sauce, teriyaki, curry, and garlic sauces.

The following assortment features combinations that, for the most part, are quickly fixed; most blend flavors better if they're prepared the evening or morning before your party. A few require more time and toil; several are best prepared just preceding dinner. These recommendations are noted with each recipe when it is important to the outcome.

Besides the sauce recipes given here, you can also purchase a number of ready-made condiments and relishes that go well with fondues. These include teriyaki sauce, ketchup, chili sauce, mustards, meat sauces, pickle relish, chutneys, and tartar sauce.

Small individual bowls or side dishes, or special fondue plates that include four or five sections for sauces, may be used for serving.

Green onions, olives, pickles, marinated artichoke hearts, pickled mushrooms, cucumber slices, and carrot and celery sticks may also be included on the table.

A Caesar or wilted lettuce salad, or simple oil and vinegar-dressed greens, accented with avocado chunks, garbanzo beans, artichoke hearts, or other ingredient favorites, complements these casual dunking dinners.

With meat or fish, you will want to include slices of crusty French or sourdough bread; some may also wish to serve a rice or potato dish as an additional accompaniment.

SAUCES FOR FONDUE 37

Blender Béarnaise Sauce

3 green onions or shallots, minced
2 tablespoons wine vinegar
2 egg yolks
1 teaspoon dried tarragon
⅛ teaspoon salt
⅛ teaspoon dry mustard
Dash of liquid hot pepper seasoning
½ cup (¼ lb.) butter, melted

The blender makes traditionally time-consuming Béarnaise go together much faster. Results are great with beef or fish fondues.

Cook onions or shallots in wine vinegar until liquid is absorbed and onion tender. Place in blender with egg yolks, dried tarragon, salt, mustard, and hot pepper seasoning. Blend for 5 seconds.

Gradually add melted butter. (If your blender does not have a small opening in the lid, cover the container with heavy foil, fasten securely with a heavy rubber band, make a hole in center of foil, and insert a funnel.) The sauce will thicken at once. If too thick, add a small amount of hot water. Makes about ¾ cup.

Cold Blender Béarnaise

3 egg yolks
2 tablespoons tarragon vinegar
2 tablespoons lemon juice
¼ teaspoon salt
2 teaspoons prepared mustard
2 medium-sized sprigs parsley
¼ teaspoon tarragon
¾ cup butter
¼ cup water

Serve this version cold. It's delicious with just about everything.

Combine egg yolks, tarragon vinegar, lemon juice, salt, mustard, parsley, and tarragon in blender container; whirl smooth.

Melt butter with water until bubbly. With blender on high, pour in hot butter in a steady stream. Sauce thickens when chilled. Serve cold. Makes 1½ cups.

Mock Béarnaise

1 teaspoon dried tarragon
1 tablespoon tarragon vinegar
1 cup mayonnaise
⅛ teaspoon dry mustard
3 peeled shallots or green onions

A simplified version of Blender Béarnaise. The main difference is the use of mayonnaise instead of the butter and egg yolks.

Soak tarragon in tarragon vinegar. Add mayonnaise, mustard, and shallots or green onions. Whirl in blender. Makes about 1¼ cups.

Sour Cream Sauce

1 tablespoon paprika (or dill weed to taste)
2 tablespoons very finely minced onion
1 cup sour cream
Salt to taste

Serve this sauce with beef, chicken, lamb, and seafood.

Combine paprika (or dill weed), onion, and sour cream. Add salt to taste. Let stand at least several hours to blend flavors. Makes about 1 cup.

Cocktail Sauce

1 very small clove garlic
½ cup sour cream
¼ cup canned tomato sauce
1 tablespoon cognac (optional)
1 tablespoon anchovy paste
1 tablespoon lemon juice
Dash of liquid hot pepper seasoning
1 teaspoon minced fresh dill (or ½ teaspoon dill weed)

Good with beef, lamb, fish, and seafood.

Purée garlic clove with a garlic press. Combine with remaining ingredients. Mix well. Chill before using. Makes about 1 cup.

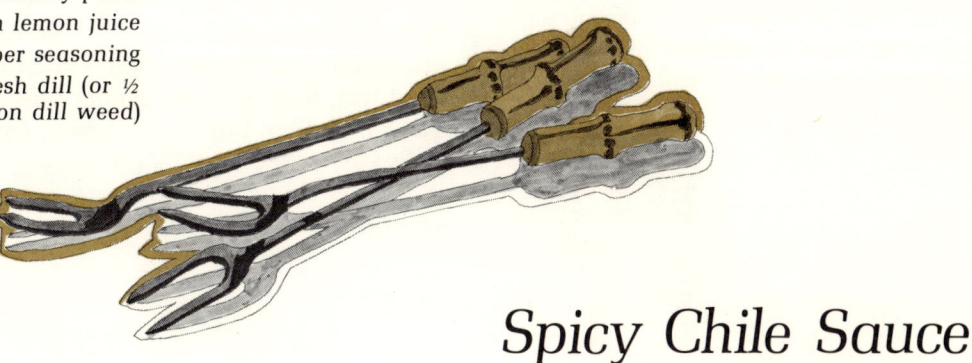

Spicy Chile Sauce

¾ cup chile sauce
½ cup chopped onion
3 tablespoons lemon juice
2 tablespoons salad oil
2 teaspoons tarragon vinegar
1 clove garlic, mashed
1 teaspoon brown sugar
½ teaspoon liquid hot pepper seasoning
¼ teaspoon dry mustard
¼ teaspoon salt

Tart and hot, this well-seasoned sauce is best with beef or fish.

Stir all ingredients together in a small pan. Heat mixture to the boiling point; simmer gently about 5 minutes. Serve hot or at room temperature. Makes about 1¼ cups.

Tartar Sauce

½ cup sour cream
½ cup unflavored yogurt
2 tablespoons pickle relish
2 tablespoons chopped parsley
1 tablespoon lemon juice
1 teaspoon chopped chives
½ teaspoon dill weed
½ teaspoon dry minced onion

The classic accompaniment for fish.

Blend ingredients. Refrigerate until serving time. Makes about 1¼ cups.

Anchovy Sauce

2 teaspoons anchovy paste (or more to taste)
⅔ cup mayonnaise

Serve with any meat, chicken, or seafood fondue—to anyone who enjoys the salty accent of anchovies.

Add anchovy paste to mayonnaise and mix well. Makes about ⅔ cup.

SAUCES FOR FONDUE

Blender Hollandaise Sauce

3 egg yolks, at room temperature
1½ tablespoons lemon juice
¾ cup butter, melted (1½ cubes)
1 tablespoon hot water
½ teaspoon salt
Dash of cayenne
1 teaspoon prepared mustard

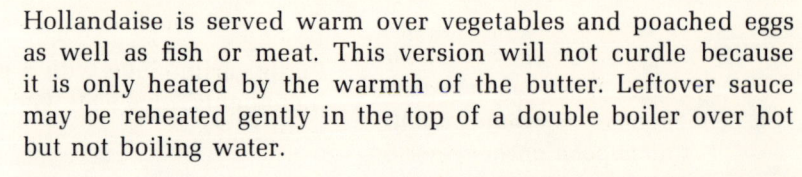

Hollandaise is served warm over vegetables and poached eggs as well as fish or meat. This version will not curdle because it is only heated by the warmth of the butter. Leftover sauce may be reheated gently in the top of a double boiler over hot but not boiling water.

Combine egg yolks and lemon juice in the blender. Melt butter and heat until it bubbles—don't brown. Add hot water to egg yolks and lemon juice; turn blender on high speed and immediately pour in the hot butter in a steady stream. (This takes about 5 seconds.)
    Add salt, cayenne, and mustard; whirl until well blended, about 30 seconds. Makes about 2 cups of sauce.

Sauce Mousseline

Combine equal amounts of Hollandaise and whipped cream. Season with a little lemon juice. (Mayonnaise may be used instead of Hollandaise.)

Blender Curry Mayonnaise

3 tablespoons lemon juice
½ teaspoon salt
1 teaspoon prepared mustard
1 teaspoon curry powder, or to taste
1 egg
1 cup salad oil

If you like curry, you'll enjoy this neatly seasoned mayonnaise.

In blender container combine lemon juice, salt, mustard, curry powder, egg, and ¼ cup salad oil. Whirl smooth.
    With blender on, slowly add ¾ cup salad oil, whirling until mixture is thick, about 2 minutes. Makes 1½ cups.

Lemon Mayonnaise Sauce

1½ cups mayonnaise
3 tablespoons lemon juice
3 tablespoons water
⅓ cup chopped green onion tops
2 cloves garlic, minced or mashed

Though especially recommended as accent to Poached Seafood and Vegetables (page 33), this sauce can be served with beef, chicken, or other seafood dishes as well.

Blend ingredients. Cover and chill until ready to serve. Divide equally among 6 bowls, or serve in one larger bowl, if preferred. Makes about 2 cups.

SAUCES FOR FONDUE

Guacamole

1 large, fully ripe avocado (10 to 12 oz.)
1 tablespoon lime or lemon juice
1 to 2 tablespoons finely minced onion or green onion
1 teaspoon minced fresh coriander (Chinese parsley or cilantro) or ¼ teaspoon ground dry coriander
1 to 2 teaspoons minced canned California green chiles (seeds and pith removed)
¼ teaspoon minced, canned small hot chile (such as jalapeno) or a few drops liquid hot pepper seasoning (optional)
Salt to taste

Versatile guacamole is a fine sauce with seafoods, meats, and vegetables.

This simple recipe, encountered in Mexico, is an authentic blending of a little tartness and a little heat combined with the butter-smooth, butter-delicate mashed avocado.

Peel and pit avocado and mash coarsely with a fork, blending in lime juice. Mix in onion to taste, coriander, green chiles, hot chile (or liquid pepper to taste), and salt to season. Serve at room temperature or chilled; cover to refrigerate up to 3 days. (To freeze, do not add onion until mixture is thawed for serving.) Makes about 1 cup guacamole.

For additional variations, try these ideas singly or in combination: Pass lime or lemon wedges to squeeze over guacamole according to taste; garnish with minced fresh coriander; add as much as ½ cup peeled, seeded, and chopped tomatoes; extend with mayonnaise or sour cream to suit taste.

Avocado Sauce

1 can (8 oz.) frozen avocado dip, thawed (or 1 small avocado, peeled and puréed in blender)
4 drops liquid hot pepper seasoning
1 tablespoon lemon juice

This goes well with Seafood Fondue (page 31). Recipe may be made from scratch—or with frozen guacamole dip and a few embellishments.

Mix thawed avocado dip (or puréed avocado) with hot pepper seasoning and lemon juice. Chill. Makes 1 cup.

Dieter's Gourmet Sauce

1 pint cottage cheese
½ pint unflavored yogurt
Dash of garlic powder
Dash of onion powder
1 teaspoon coarse (kosher-style) salt
About 1 teaspoon mixed fresh herbs, finely chopped (suggest about ¼ teaspoon each parsley, lemon thyme, oregano, winter savory, or others as available—or use about ⅛ teaspoon each of the dried herbs)
3 teaspoons tarragon wine vinegar, or to taste

This low-fat sauce remains fluffy and flavorful for a week under refrigeration. The combination complements chicken and fish or seafood cooked either in broth or oil.

Put cottage cheese in an electric mixer or blender and beat or blend until smooth. Add yogurt, garlic and onion powder, salt, chopped fresh herbs, and wine vinegar. Beat or blend until well blended. Store in refrigerator—it is better the second day. Makes about 2½ cups sauce.

For variety, crumble about ¼ cup Roquefort or blue cheese into about ⅓ of the mixture.

Sauce Rémoulade

½ cup sour cream
½ cup mayonnaise
¼ cup finely chopped dill pickles
1 tablespoon finely chopped capers
½ tablespoon prepared mustard
½ tablespoon finely chopped shallots
1 teaspoon chopped parsley
¼ teaspoon tarragon
¼ teaspoon chervil

Fish or poultry benefit from an accent with this sauce.

Mix all ingredients. Makes about 1¼ cups. Store in refrigerator.

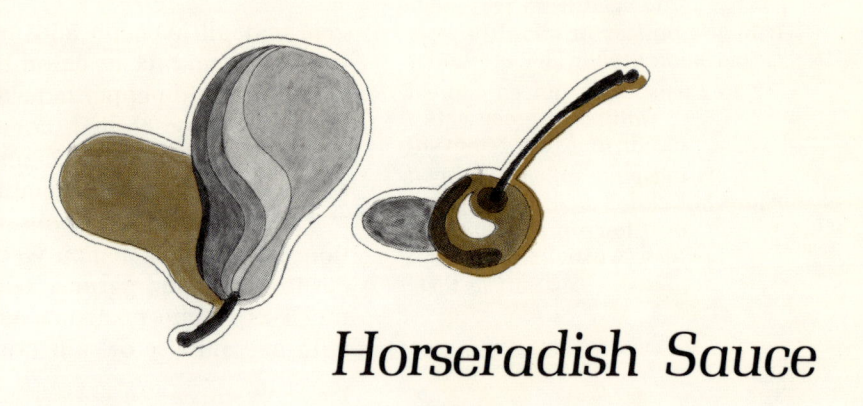

Horseradish Sauce

1 cup sour cream
2 to 3 teaspoons prepared horseradish (to taste)
½ teaspoon lemon juice
Few drops Worcestershire
Dash of salt and pepper

Make this as mild—or wild—as you wish. It is especially good with seafoods.

Stir ingredients together. Adjust seasonings to taste. Refrigerate until serving time. Makes about 1 cup.

Whipped Horseradish Cream

2 hard-cooked eggs, shelled
1 teaspoon Dijon-style mustard
½ teaspoon prepared horseradish
¼ teaspoon dill weed
Salt
½ cup whipping cream

Fine with fish; interesting with lamb. Try it, too, with beef.

Mash eggs finely with a fork, then blend in thoroughly the mustard, horseradish, dill weed, and salt to taste.

Whip the cream just until it's stiff but still will mound softly. Fold in the seasoned eggs. Serve sauce at once (or chill, covered, for as long as two or three hours); blend before serving. Makes about 1 cup.

Chutney Sauce

¾ cup sour cream
1 teaspoon curry powder (or to taste)
¼ cup chutney, chopped or puréed in blender

Bright accent with lamb, beef, chicken, or seafood fondues.

Mix together sour cream, curry powder, and chutney. Chill to blend flavors. Remove from refrigerator about 15 minutes before serving. Makes 1 cup.

Tomato Lemon Chutney

1 tablespoon salad oil
1 small whole dried red chile pepper
½ teaspoon cumin seed
½ teaspoon mustard seed
¼ teaspoon nutmeg
1 pound can whole tomatoes and juice
½ cup currants
½ cup sugar
½ lemon, finely chopped (including peel)

In a saucepan combine salad oil, chile pepper, cumin seed, mustard seed, and nutmeg. Heat, stirring, until the seeds start to pop and jump.

Stir in tomatoes and juice, currants, sugar, and lemon. Boil rapidly, stirring frequently to break up tomato, until very thick. Cover and chill.

This sauce is best made 3 or 4 days before use. Makes about 1⅓ cups.

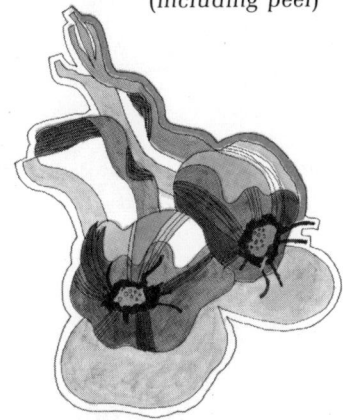

Flavored Butters

These four flavored butters may be made ahead and refrigerated. Set them out at room temperature to soften slightly before serving. For added interest, try rolling them into balls or use one of the fancy molds available in various shapes and designs.

Garlic Butter

½ cup (¼ lb.) softened butter
1 small clove of garlic, puréed
Cayenne or Worcestershire to taste

Excellent accent to beef, lamb. A garlic-lover will think it's perfect with almost anything.

Cream butter with garlic; add cayenne or Worcestershire to taste.

Mustard Butter

¼ cup prepared mustard
½ cup (¼ lb.) softened butter

Blend ingredients. Let stand several hours to blend flavors.

Blue Cheese Butter

1 package (4 oz.) blue cheese
½ cup (¼ lb.) softened butter

Blend cheese and butter. Let stand several hours so flavors blend.

Toasted Onion Butter

1 teaspoon toasted dried onions
¼ teaspoon salt
¼ teaspoon Worcestershire
½ cup (¼ lb.) softened butter

Combine ingredients. Let stand in the refrigerator or at room temperature for several hours to let the flavors blend thoroughly.

SAUCES FOR FONDUE

Teriyaki Sauce

½ cup canned bouillon
3 tablespoons soy sauce
2 teaspoons lemon juice
2 teaspoons dry Sherry
2 teaspoons honey
¼ teaspoon garlic powder
½ teaspoon ground ginger

Teriyaki flavor complements beef, chicken, lamb, or seafood—and makes a delicious sauce for raw or cooked mushrooms. If you can stand the wait, let each bit of cooked food stand in the marinade while your next morsel is cooking. The additional flavor picked up makes it worthwhile.

Combine all ingredients and heat to boiling. Serve warm or cold. Makes about ¾ cup.

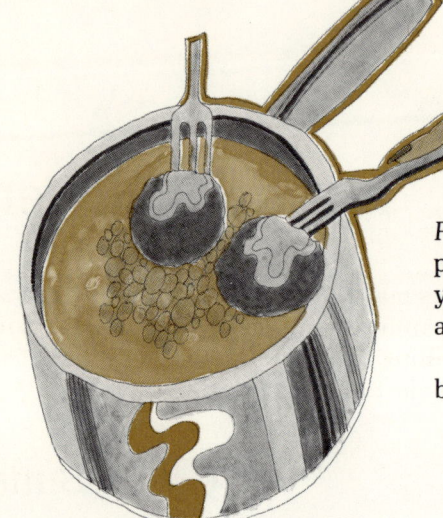

Pesto

Pesto is actually just an innocent-looking, quickly made, green paste of basil, Parmesan cheese, and olive oil . . . relatively mild, yet a delight when blended into butter or made into mayonnaise and paired with beef, chicken, seafood, and vegetable fondues.

If you don't have a supply of fresh basil, you can make the basic pesto sauce with frozen pesto, available in many stores.

Basic Pesto Sauce

2 cups packed fresh basil leaves, washed and drained well
1 cup freshly grated Parmesan cheese
½ cup olive oil

Put basil in a blender jar; add cheese and oil and cover. Turning motor on and off, whirl at high speed until a very coarse purée is formed; push pesto down from sides of blender jar frequently with a rubber spatula. Use at once, cover and refrigerate up to a week, or freeze in small portions. The surface will darken when exposed to air, so stir the pesto just before using. Makes about 1⅓ cups.

Pesto Mayonnaise

1 egg
2 tablespoons lemon juice
1 clove garlic
½ cup basic pesto sauce or frozen pesto (defrosted)
½ cup melted butter
¾ cup salad oil

In a blender jar combine egg, lemon juice, and garlic. Cover and whirl at high speed until blended. Turn motor off, add basic pesto sauce, then turn on high speed and gradually pour in butter and salad oil. For pouring or dipping consistency sauce, serve at once or at room temperature; for a thicker sauce, cover, chill. Makes about 2 cups.

Pesto Butter

3 tablespoons basic pesto sauce or frozen pesto (defrosted)
½ cup soft butter

Blend pesto sauce with butter. Makes ⅔ cup.

Red Wine Sauce

½ cup chopped onion
3 tablespoons butter
1 teaspoon flour
1 cup dry red table wine
1 clove garlic, mashed
1 tablespoon tomato purée

Most agreeable with beef or lamb.

Sauté onion in butter until lightly browned. Stir in flour, cook another minute, then add wine, garlic, and tomato purée. Simmer 15 minutes and serve hot (place in dessert fondue dish over candle warmer or electric trivet).

Curry Dip

½ cup sour cream
3 tablespoons mayonnaise
½ teaspoon curry powder (or to taste, depending upon brand and strength)
⅛ teaspoon cayenne pepper
1 tablespoon catsup
¼ teaspoon Worcestershire
Dash of salt
Juice of 1 clove garlic

Highly recommended as an accompaniment to Chicken-Mushroom Fondue (page 35), although a similar combination was originally discovered in London as a dip for raw vegetables.

Combine ingredients. Refrigerate several hours or overnight to allow flavors to blend. Stir again before serving. Makes about 1 cup.

Tempura Sauce

The traditional accompaniment to tempura (page 32), this sauce begins with a broth (*Dashi*) made of dried bonito fish and dried tangle seaweed.

The easiest way to prepare it is to buy packages labeled "Da-shi-no-Moto soup stock." These come in two forms—bags like tea bags containing the ingredients, or pellets like bouillon cubes. Most of these packages give you instructions in English for brewing the Dashi.

To make it with the tea-bag type, you just drop one ¾ oz. bag in 3 cups of boiling water and simmer about 5 minutes. Remove the bag (don't mash it or the broth will be cloudy) and you have Dashi.

To make sauce, combine in a pan 3 cups prepared Dashi, fish stock or chicken broth; 1 cup soy sauce; and 1 cup rice wine (sake), Sherry, or sweet rice wine (mirin). Bring to a boil, and remove from heat. Serve hot in individual bowls. Makes enough for 6 people.

SAUCES FOR FONDUE

Veal with a Swiss touch (page 59) is a simple combination of meat in a wine sauce, served flambé.

46 CHAFING DISH ENTREES

Chafing Dish Entrees...
Elementary to Elegant

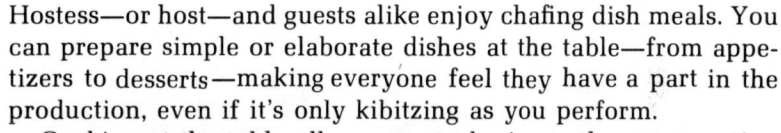

Hostess—or host—and guests alike enjoy chafing dish meals. You can prepare simple or elaborate dishes at the table—from appetizers to desserts—making everyone feel they have a part in the production, even if it's only kibitzing as you perform.

Cooking at the table allows you to be in on the conversation and out of the kitchen, and it enables you to serve the food without any delay.

Before we can talk knowledgeably about chafing dishes, we have to agree on the meaning of the term.

The original meaning was *to make warm*, from the French *chauffer*. The definition today is much broader and more encompassing, referring to any pan or vessel placed over a source of heat to warm or cook food at the table.

Chafing dishes are available as complete units, or you can purchase pans and burners separately for increased versatility (see the discussion beginning on page 5 about various pans).

The complete units are actually portable double boilers: They have a burner, stand, water pan (bain-marie), a cooking pan (blazer), and lid.

The blazer pan is used directly over the flame for cooking foods requiring higher temperatures—browning, setting eggs, sautéing fruits. If you cook something you would normally prepare in the top of a double boiler, cook it in the blazer pan over the water bath.

The water bath is also used for holding foods—keeping them hot on buffet or dinner table without further cooking.

When selecting your equipment, choose a dish of heavy metal; pans made of thin metal tend to scorch foods easily, or heat only the middle that is directly over the flame.

The most expensive chafing dishes are made of sterling silver. Unless the equipment is going to be used regularly, this is probably too costly (and formal) for most homes. Copper or stainless steel pans with tin, cast iron, or silver linings are hospitable-looking and have excellent cooking qualities.

CHAFING DISH ENTREES 47

Probably most practical with respect to cooking and cleaning are stainless steel (grade 18/8 is best), porcelain or enamel-coated cast iron, or a good grade of aluminum.

For a discussion of the various kinds of fuel, please turn back to page 6.

Once the equipment is purchased, the rest is up to the cook. The secret to success now is *organization*.

Be selective in choosing a recipe for at-the-table presentation. Especially if you are a novice, use a recipe designed for the chafing dish. Later on you can be more inventive.

You should create the illusion that the dish you prepare requires little effort. To do this, arrange a work tray with all the necessary ingredients ready to use, possibly extra fuel (although denatured alcohol should be added in the kitchen), and a small towel.

If the dish is long-cooking or complicated, do the major preparation in the kitchen, leaving only the heating and last-minute additions to do at the table.

Some foods must be previously prepared, some only half prepared, but all must be in a stage of preparation that allows you to execute the finished dish within the shortest space of time and with the greatest of ease.

For a smooth performance, you should rehearse step-by-step, timing yourself, checking for adequate serving containers and utensils on your work tray, determining what should be prepared in advance. If purchasing the food for practice seems extravagant, at least do a dry run. You might even contemplate your commentary, if you think this is necessary, but not to the point where it begins to sound like a speech.

The recipes in the section are divided into several basic categories. Eggs are a natural since they require moderate heat and can be adapted in many ways into entrees that are appropriate for brunches, lunches, and midnight suppers.

Omelets work beautifully in an omelet pan over direct heat. When four people are gathered and hunger sets in, this is a perfect way to quell the pangs—simple to do, fun to watch, delicious to eat.

Meatballs, which are merely served from your chafing dish after preparation has been completed in the kitchen, is also a good choice for company gatherings when you want the service to be special.

The meat entrees—Steak Diane, Scallopini Picatte, Beef Medallions—require intense heat to brown quickly. Just remember to have the flame full blast and your pan preheated. If the temperature is too low, the meat will not brown properly, lose juices, and, in general, not be a thing of beauty to cook or serve. If your burner doesn't emit sufficient heat, it would be best to substitute your electric frying pan.

Chicken and seafood entrees close this section with a selection of easy-to-do main dishes that will delight both the hostess and guests alike.

For special beginnings—appetizers and hors d'oeuvres—and flamboyant finales—fancy desserts—turn to the separate chapters on pages 11 and 67, respectively.

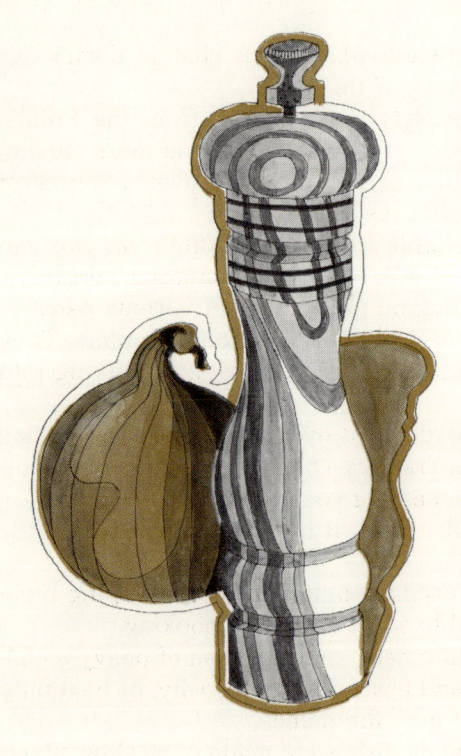

Nut-Crusted Oysters and Eggs

1 jar (10 oz.) small Pacific oysters, drained
½ teaspoon salt
1 egg
1 tablespoon water
1 cup very finely chopped walnuts or filberts
½ cup flour
6 slices chopped bacon
8 eggs
1 teaspoon Worcestershire
2 or 3 dashes liquid hot pepper seasoning
2 tablespoons brandy
About 1 tablespoon chopped chives

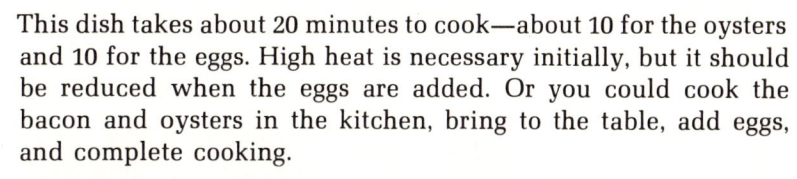

This dish takes about 20 minutes to cook—about 10 for the oysters and 10 for the eggs. High heat is necessary initially, but it should be reduced when the eggs are added. Or you could cook the bacon and oysters in the kitchen, bring to the table, add eggs, and complete cooking.

Sprinkle oysters with salt. Beat the 1 egg with water; add oysters. In a bag combine nuts and flour; lift oysters from egg with fork, a few at a time, and drop into bag. Shake to coat well. Arrange oysters in a single layer on a small tray; sprinkle any remaining nut mixture over them. Cover lightly and chill at least 30 minutes.

At the table, in a wide frying pan (about 12-inch diameter), cook the bacon over medium-high heat until crisp. Remove bacon and reserve.

To drippings, add the oysters and brown on each side; do not crowd. (If necessary, remove a few of the cooked oysters from the pan to make room for the remaining shellfish.)

While oysters are cooking, break the 8 eggs into a bowl and beat with Worcestershire and liquid hot pepper seasoning.

Add brandy to oysters and set aflame; pour the eggs into pan, pouring around the oysters as much as possible. Cook eggs until set; slide a wide spatula under oysters to let eggs flow to bottom of pan. Reduce or extinguish heat.

Cut a few spears of chives from a potted chive plant and snip over the oysters (or used chopped chives); sprinkle with the cooked bacon, and serve. Makes 4 generous servings.

Scrambled Eggs and Smoked Salmon on Toast

¼ cup chopped chives or green onions
¼ cup soft butter
⅔ cup shredded Swiss cheese
6 slices whole wheat toast
About 12 slices smoked salmon
6 eggs
2 tablespoons light cream or milk
1½ tablespoons butter
Salt and pepper to taste

This dish is equally appropriate day or night. Smoked salmon slices are lightly layered atop toast, which has been spread with a mixture of Swiss cheese, butter, and chives, and then covered with lightly scrambled eggs.

Combine chives, soft butter, and cheese; spread on toast. Top each slice with slices of smoked salmon. Keep warm on plates in the oven.

Beat together eggs and cream. Melt the butter in a frying pan or chafing dish. Bring to the table and place over direct flame.

When the butter begins to bubble and brown slightly, add egg mixture and cook, stirring, until just softly scrambled. Season to taste with salt and pepper (salt very lightly if salmon is salty). Turn off heating unit.

Bring plates with toast and salmon to the table. Top salmon with the scrambled eggs. Serves 3 to 6.

CHAFING DISH ENTREES

Creamy Crab-Egg Scramble

½ cup milk
¼ teaspoon pepper
1 can (6 oz.) white sauce
8 eggs
¼ cup (⅛ lb.) butter
1 package (3 oz.) cream cheese with chives, diced
2 cups crab meat (or 2 cans, about 7 oz. each, drained)

For a breakfast or brunch menu, agreeable companions to this dish might be broiled grapefruit, sweet rolls, and cafe au lait. The eggs will hold about 20 minutes if there is a delay.

With fork or wire whisk, beat together milk, pepper, and white sauce; with a fork beat in eggs, two or three at a time, until mixture is a smooth yellow.

Melt butter in a chafing dish over direct flame (or in electric fry pan over low heat). Pour in egg mixture; when mixture begins to set, lift it from pan with a spatula (avoid constant stirring).

While eggs are still fluid, stir in cream cheese. Cook until set but still quite moist. Reduce heat; add crab meat, drained; cover and warm 5 minutes. Serve at once. Serves 4.

Eggs Rancheros

1 can (10 oz.) enchilada sauce
2 tablespoons dried bell pepper (optional)
4 eggs
2 English muffins, halved, toasted, buttered

This aromatic entree is especially simple since canned enchilada sauce is the ready-made base in which the eggs cook. Have English muffins toasted, buttered, and ready in a basket alongside the frying pan.

In a large frying pan over direct flame, heat enchilada sauce with green pepper, if desired.

Carefully break eggs, one at a time, into the bubbling sauce. Cover pan, lower heat, and cook until eggs are set.

Serve each egg on top of a toasted English muffin half, with some of the sauce spooned over. Makes 4 servings of 1 egg each.

Tomatoes and Eggs Italian

3 or 4 large tomatoes
3 tablespoons butter or margarine
1 pound mushrooms, sliced
6 or 8 eggs
Salt and pepper
¾ cup shredded Swiss or Cheddar cheese

This quick dish of eggs poached in a fresh tomato and mushroom mixture has an Italian accent. For brunch, round out the menu by serving a platter of coppa (Italian sausage) and figs for starters, thin melba toast as an accompaniment; for midnight supper, serve with rosé wine and a crisp salad.

Peel tomatoes, cut in cubes, and let drain for several minutes.

Meanwhile, over direct heat in butter or margarine sauté mushrooms about 5 minutes. Stir in tomatoes and heat to simmering. Bring to table with eggs and cheese.

At the table, use a spoon to make 6 or 8 nest spaces and break an egg in each space. Season with salt and pepper, top with shredded cheese. Cover pan and cook until eggs are set. Serves 3 or 4.

Eggs Fried With Prawns and Dill

2 tablespoons butter
½ teaspoon salt
¼ teaspoon dill weed
1 pound prawns or large shrimp (40 to the pound), shelled and deveined
4 eggs
2 tablespoons heavy cream
Sherry (about 2 teaspoons)

Have the butter, salt, and dill in the cooking pan when you bring it to the table. The cleaned shrimp can be in one bowl, the whole eggs in another, and the cream in a small pitcher. A small salad-dressing bottle works fine as a miniature decanter for Sherry. You'll need a wide spatula for serving.

Melt butter with salt and dill in a wide pan over direct heat. Add the prawns and cook, stirring, just until they begin to turn pink, about 2 minutes. Make 4 spaces among the prawns and break an egg into each spot. Pour cream over eggs; cover pan and cook until eggs are set to suit your taste. Pass Sherry and let each person drizzle about ½ teaspoon over each egg. Makes 2 to 4 servings.

Curried Eggs with Avocado

6 eggs
½ teaspoon salt
Dash pepper
1½ teaspoons Worcestershire
3 tablespoons cream or milk
½ ripe (but firm) avocado
1 tablespoon lemon juice
1 tablespoon butter or margarine
2 tablespoons minced onion
½ teaspoon curry powder

Here's an interesting way to embellish eggs. Try it for brunch or a late evening supper with crisp toast and bacon or sausage.

In a bowl lightly beat the eggs with salt, pepper, Worcestershire, and cream. Peel avocado and cut crosswise slices; drizzle with the lemon juice; set aside.
    In a frying pan or blazer pan heat butter; add onion and curry powder and cook, stirring, over medium flame for 2 or 3 minutes. Add egg mixture and cook slowly, stirring lightly, until softly scrambled. Turn off heat; serve, arranging avocado slices over top. Makes 2 very generous, 3 average, or 4 small servings.

Shrimp Chow Dun

1 cup diced raw shrimp
½ cup sliced mushrooms, canned or fresh
½ cup chopped onion
½ cup thawed frozen peas, uncooked
2 tablespoons salad oil
6 eggs
½ teaspoon salt
Pepper

Prepare shrimp, mushrooms, and onions in advance. The rest of this Chinese egg dish is very easy.

In frying pan cook shrimp and vegetables for 3 to 5 minutes in heated oil over direct high flame.
    To the eggs, add salt, and some pepper; beat just enough to mix.
    Pour eggs over the vegetables, distributing them as evenly as possible. Turn heat low, and cook just until the eggs begin to set. They should be moist and creamy. Serve at once. Makes 4 servings.

CHAFING DISH ENTREES

Tortillas Con Hongos

3 tablespoons butter
¼ pound mushrooms, chopped, including stems
½ cup finely minced onion
1 small clove garlic, minced or mashed (optional)
4 eggs, beaten
¼ teaspoon salt
Dash of pepper
¾ to 1 cup finely diced jack cheese
Tortilla chips or crisply fried tortilla strips

Tortillas, mushrooms, and eggs make a marvelous combination. As a base for the softly scrambled eggs, use packaged snack chips, slightly broken, or refrigerated flour or corn tortilla shells cut in strips and fried in butter.

Melt butter in a frying pan over direct heat. Combine mushrooms, onion, and garlic, and cook in butter over medium heat until liquid is evaporated, about 10 to 15 minutes.

Have ready in a bowl, eggs, salt, pepper, and cheese. Add to mushroom mixture. Cook, lifting and stirring gently (almost like cooking a French omelet), until eggs are set but still soft.

Serve on tortilla chips or over crisply fried tortilla strips, which have been warmed in the oven. Makes 2 generous servings. (For 4 smaller servings, increase eggs to 6.)

Ham and Scrambled Eggs

6 eggs
2 tablespoons water
1½ tablespoons chopped canned green chiles (or more, to taste), seeds and pith removed
1½ cups finely diced cooked ham
Dash of pepper
2 tablespoons butter or margarine
1 cup shredded jack cheese

Easy to fix in cramped quarters, this substantial dish of scrambled eggs, diced ham, shredded jack cheese, and chopped green chiles works beautifully in a chafing dish.

With a fork, beat together eggs, water, chiles, ham, and pepper.

In a frying pan over direct flame, heat butter; pour eggs into pan and cook over low heat, stirring until eggs are almost set.

Sprinkle cheese over egg mixture, cover, and cook until cheese melts. Serves 3 or 4.

Confetti Eggs

½ medium-sized green pepper, diced
½ cup minced onion
2 tablespoons salad oil
6 medium-sized fresh mushrooms, thinly sliced
2 tablespoons minced parsley
1½ teaspoons salt
¼ teaspoon pepper
½ teaspoon mixed salad herbs (or basil or oregano)
½ teaspoon Worcestershire
6 eggs, slightly beaten
2 tablespoons butter or margarine
2 large fresh tomatoes, peeled, diced, and seedy portions removed

Fresh vegetables and special seasonings add color and flavor to scrambled eggs. Baked or fried ham and fresh pineapple slices might be served with this brunch, lunch, or dinner.

In the kitchen: In a saucepan or frying pan, sauté green pepper and onion in salad oil until slightly soft but not browned, about 5 minutes.

Add mushrooms, parsley, 1 teaspoon of the salt, ⅛ teaspoon of the pepper, herbs, and Worcestershire. Cook slowly, stirring occasionally, for about 10 minutes. Green pepper should still be bright green. Remove from heat. Beat remaining ½ teaspoon salt and ⅛ teaspoon pepper into eggs.

At the table: Over direct flame, heat butter in another frying pan; add eggs, and cook, stirring gently with a wide spatula, until eggs begin to set.

Add mushroom mixture and the tomatoes; stir gently until eggs are softly scrambled. Serve immediately. Makes 3 to 4 servings.

Lobster La Flamberge

3 tablespoons butter
8 eggs
2 tablespoons sour cream
3 tablespoons dry vermouth
½ teaspoon salt
About 1 cup sliced cooked lobster meat (meat from 1 tail)
¼ cup small, cooked shrimp, shelled and deveined
1 to 2 tablespoons sliced almonds

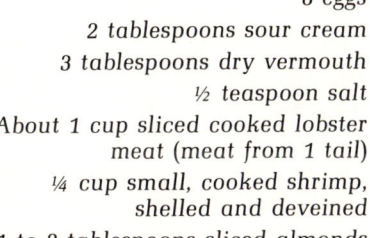

To prepare this dish with flair, bring the eggs to the table in a basket and crack them into a bowl that contains the sour cream blended with the vermouth and salt.

Have the lobster split lengthwise and the tail meat freed and cut in chunks; return meat to the shell and use it as serving container until you are ready to add lobster to the eggs, along with the shrimp and almonds. Two eggs are reserved until last, for breaking over the dish—to glaze and moisten the shellfish and the cooked eggs.

Melt butter in a wide shallow pan over direct heat. While it is heating, break 6 eggs into a bowl containing the sour cream blended with vermouth and salt; beat in the eggs.

Pour eggs into sizzling butter and cook, stirring gently from the bottom as eggs set.

While eggs are still fairly fluid, add lobster, shrimp, and almonds. When eggs are set, break the 2 remaining eggs into pan; stir to moisten and glaze all. Cook for a few seconds longer, then serve directly to 3 or 4 persons.

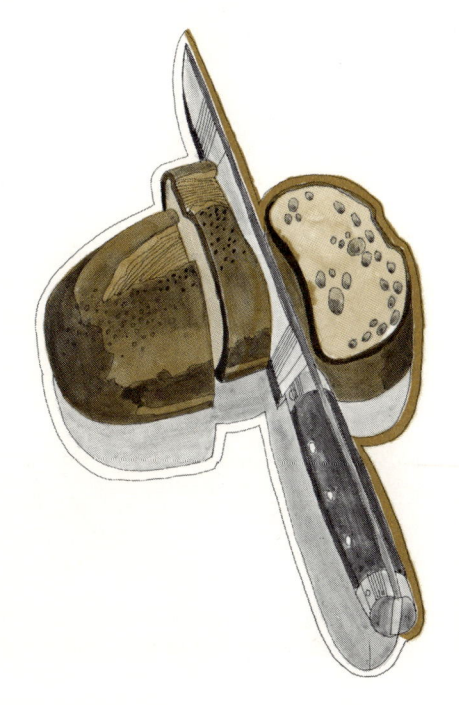

The Art of the Omelet

When you master an omelet, the door is opened to a whole range of recipes that will do quadruple duty as breakfast, brunch, lunch, or midnight supper.

Just add a few trimmings—cheese, mushrooms, olives, onion, green pepper, bacon, ham, shrimp, avocado, tomato, jam, jelly, marmalade—and you have the basis for interesting egg dishes.

In spite of its simplicity, the art of making an omelet requires concentration and practice. An improperly made omelet ends up overcooked, burned, or scrambled. The perfect omelet is tender and golden, firm but delicate outside, smooth and creamy inside.

The Pan-Egg Ratio. The size and shape of your omelet pan should determine the number of eggs going into it. A pan with longer-than-usual handle and upcurved edges make manipulation easier.

By measuring the diameter of the rim, you will know the number of eggs that should be used for each omelet: 6 to 6½ inches for one egg and 7 to 8½ inches for two-egg omelets. A two-egg omelet is a good individual size and the easiest size to handle over a chafing dish heating element.

Breaking and Beating. It takes very little equipment and few ingredients to make an omelet.

Basic proportions to tuck away in your memory are:
- 1 teaspoon of water for each egg
- A little salt (⅛ teaspoon for every two eggs)
- A dash of pepper

CHAFING DISH ENTREES

Omelet con't

Break eggs for one omelet into a bowl; add water, salt, and pepper. Beat vigorously with a fork for about 30 seconds, or until yolks and whites are blended.

Heating the Pan. Adjust the heat to medium high on a butane burning unit or maximum heat on units using denatured alcohol or canned heat. Place the pan over the cooking unit to heat while you mix the first omelet. For two-egg omelet, add 2 teaspoons butter or margarine (1 teaspoon per egg) to the pan—if the pan is hot enough it will sizzle and foam. Heat until the foam begins to subside.

Pour in Eggs. Pour beaten eggs all at once into heated pan. They should begin to set and turn opaque around the edges almost immediately. Slide pan rapidly back and forth across the burner, keeping omelet in motion and free from the bottom of the pan.

Shake it, Lift Edge. As soon as the bottom of the omelet begins to set, slip a thin-bladed spatula well under the edges and let the uncooked eggs flow into contact with the center of the pan. This lifting, along with frequent shaking, causes the rippled surface and irregular edges that are characteristic of a good omelet.

The most important thing to remember is that the omelet should never brown; it should be the same color outside as it is inside. Don't be discouraged if initial attempts turn out lightly browned; it just takes practice.

Don't worry about tearing the omelet as you lift the edges; the fresh supply of liquid egg soon mends the damage.

The omelet is done when the egg no longer runs freely but the top still looks liquid and creamy. If you're going to add a filling, do so now. For a three-egg omelet, spoon about 2 tablespoons filling in the center directly in line with the handle. Don't try to add too much filling because it complicates folding the omelet out of the pan.

Removing from Pan. Fold omelet in thirds, flipping it onto the plate with the final fold. Garnish with additional filling, if desired.

Mushroom-Cashew Medley

1½ teaspoons cornstarch
1 teaspoon water
⅓ cup sour cream
¼ cup (⅛ lb.) butter or margarine
½ pound mushrooms, thinly sliced
⅓ cup salted cashews, coarsely chopped
2 cloves garlic, minced or mashed

This dish enhances a meat course of roast or chops, or stands alone as the menu vegetable. Prepare while roast is firming up or as chops complete cooking.

Smoothly blend cornstarch with water; stir with sour cream until combined. Set aside.

Melt butter in a large frying pan or chafing dish over medium heat. Add mushrooms, and, stirring frequently, cook until limp and tan in color, about 4 minutes. Add chopped cashews and garlic; stir and fry an additional 2 minutes.

Add sour cream mixture to mushroom mixture; stir constantly over heat until cream is heated to simmering point. Turn flame low and serve from chafing dish. Makes 4 servings.

Bruncheon Mushrooms

4 tablespoons butter
1 small onion, finely diced
1 pound fresh mushrooms, sliced through with stems attached
1 tablespoon flour
1 teaspoon paprika
Salt and pepper to taste
⅓ cup dry vermouth
1½ cups sour cream
1 teaspoon lemon juice

With mushrooms on the menu, the rest of the meal seems to take on more elegance. This sauce, accented with vermouth and sour cream, is served over English muffins or rice, and is ideal for brunch or lunch.

In the kitchen: Melt butter in a frying pan or chafing dish; then sauté onion over high heat until golden. Add mushrooms and sauté until they are moist. Stir in the flour, paprika, salt, and pepper and cook until bubbly.

Bring to the table and place over direct flame. Have vermouth, sour cream, and lemon juice measured and on your work tray.

Gradually stir in the vermouth and cook until thickened. Mix in the sour cream and lemon juice. Heat gently but thoroughly. (Do not let the sauce boil.) Serve over lightly toasted English muffins or hot cooked rice. Makes about 6 servings.

Quick Sukiyaki

1½ pounds top round steak or sirloin, 1 to 2 inches thick
4 small white boiling onions
2 bunches green onions
2 green peppers
1 small head celery
¼ pound fresh mushrooms or 1 can (6 oz.) sliced mushrooms
1 pound spinach
½ cup soy sauce
1 bouillon cube
½ cup water
2 tablespoons sugar
1 to 2 inch beef suet

The traditional sukiyaki dinner is a ceremony. This is a simplified version—all ingredients are available from your neighborhood grocer—but it's best cooked at the table as the Japanese do. Use an electric frying pan, a good-sized skillet over a butane burner, or a wok on a hibachi (this is best done outdoors).

Most tedious part of the recipe is the preparation of the vegetables, but all the work is done ahead of time.

In the kitchen: Trim any fat from meat. Using a very sharp knife, cut meat across grain in slices ⅛ to 1/16 inch thick. (If slices are large, halve or quarter them to make bite-size pieces.)

Cut white onions into eighths; slice green onions lengthwise, then cut crosswise in 1½-inch strips.

Seed green peppers and cut in small strips lengthwise.

Slice celery diagonally in ½-inch-wide strips.

Slice mushrooms, including stems, lengthwise in pieces ⅛ inch thick, or drain canned mushrooms.

Wash spinach, remove stems, and cut large leaves in half.

Mix together in a pitcher soy, bouillon cube which has been dissolved in the ½ cup water, and sugar.

To start the first batch of sukiyaki, stir suet in the pan until pan is well coated with fat; remove browned suet.

At the table: Add one-half of the meat; cook over medium-high heat (or direct high flame) until meat is brown; push to one corner of the pan.

Add half the white onions, green pepper, and celery; stir lightly.

Add half the soy mixture and, stirring often, cook rapidly for 5 minutes. Stir in half the green onions and mushrooms and cook for 1 minute. Mix in half the spinach and cook for 1 minute.

Serve at once with rice.

This recipe serves 4 with plenty for seconds.

CHAFING DISH ENTREES 55

Beef Medallions Sauté with Wild Rice

4 small beef fillet steaks (about ⅓ inch thick and about ⅓ pound each)
Salt
2 tablespoons butter
¼ teaspoon ground sage
¼ teaspoon basil
½ teaspoon prepared English (hot) mustard or Dijon-style mustard
1 package (6 oz.) wild rice mix, cooked according to package directions, or 2 to 3 cups hot cooked white, brown, or wild rice
⅓ cup dry white wine
2 teaspoons capers (optional)
1 or 2 tablespoons thinly sliced green onions, white part only (optional)

When dinner hour is unpredictable and you're in a party mood, have everything ready ahead of time and you can quickly sauté this entree.

Beef served atop rice only needs a green salad as accompaniment; add a dessert from the freezer or a favorite pastry shop.

Sprinkle the meat lightly with salt. Heat medium-sized crêpe pan or frying pan over direct high heat from butane burner or other table top burner which provides good heat. Melt 1 tablespoon of the butter and quickly stir in the sage, basil, and mustard. Add the meat and brown until done as you prefer, figuring approximately 3 minutes to a side for rare steak.

Place meat on a bed of the rice and keep warm.

To the frying pan, add the remaining 1 tablespoon butter and the wine; boil rapidly, stirring occasionally, until reduced about half. Add capers. Pour juices over meat and rice; sprinkle with green onions. Makes 4 servings.

Steak Au Poivre

2 tender steaks, ½ inch thick, well trimmed
Whole black peppers
2 minced shallots or green onions
2 tablespoons beef fat or salad oil
About 3 ounces cognac
3 tablespoons red wine, cream, or beef broth

Even people who are partial to thick, thick steaks will approve of this pepper-laden version using a thin cut of any tender steak. High heat is essential, so it might be wise to preheat blazer pan or frying pan over the range prior to placing it atop canned heat or alcohol.

Coarsely crush some whole peppers with the rolling pin (if you put them in a plastic bag first, you'll have no trouble) and press them into both sides of the steak with your hands (you'll need about 1 teaspoon to a steak).

Have the pan hot. Sauté shallots or onions in oil. When the shallots are tender, push to one side and add the steaks. Cook quickly on one side, turn and cook the other. When the steaks are done to your liking, pour in cognac and ignite. As soon as the flames die down, put meat on heated plates and add wine to pan. Scrape up pan crispings and ladle over steaks. Makes 2 servings.

Steak Diane

¼ cup (⅛ lb.) butter or margarine
2 to 2½ pounds beef fillet or other tender boneless steak, cut ½ inch thick
2 tablespoons fresh lemon juice
1 tablespoon Worcestershire
2 tablespoons chopped chives (or onion tops)
2 tablespoons chopped parsley
Parsley and lemon wedges for garnish

A fresh lemon usually has about 3 tablespoons of juice. Practice on a few and you'll soon know just how much to squeeze directly over this steak. If the lemon seems seedy, it's a good idea to wrap cheesecloth over it.

To accompany Steak Diane, you'll want to serve foods that do not require last minute preparation and that can be kept warm at the table while the meat cooks. Hot buttered noodles and a green or yellow vegetable will keep warm in covered dishes. A crisp green salad, bread sticks, and a fruit dessert might complete the menu.

Using an electric frying pan or other frying pan or chafing dish over high flame, melt butter or margarine. Put in meat and brown quickly on both sides; cook to desired doneness, about 3 to 6 minutes. Remove meat to a heated platter.

Add lemon juice, Worcestershire, chives, and parsley to the pan; stir together. Pour sauce at once over the steaks; garnish with parsley and lemon wedges. Makes 4 to 6 servings.

Joe's Special

2 pounds ground beef chuck, crumbled
2 tablespoons olive oil or salad oil
2 medium-sized onions, finely chopped
2 cloves garlic, minced or mashed
½ pound mushrooms, sliced (optional)
1¼ teaspoons salt
¼ teaspoon nutmeg
¼ teaspoon pepper
¼ teaspoon oregano
1 package (10 oz.) frozen chopped spinach, thawed and well drained, or ½ pound fresh spinach, washed, drained, and chopped (about 4 cups)
4 to 6 eggs

No one is quite sure of the origin of the one-dish meal called Joe's Special. A staple of several San Francisco restaurants, it has been popular in that city for several generations.

According to various accounts, it was created as an after-hours snack by dance band musicians of the 1920's; by a legendary restaurant chef as a quick-cooking Italian frittata; and by miners who frequented the Barbary Coast.

Simple to prepare from easily available ingredients—ground beef, spinach, and eggs—the dish remains a favorite. You can serve Joe's Special for a quick supper or snack, but hearty eaters will enjoy it for brunch or late-evening repast—particularly when it's prepared on the spot in a chafing dish over direct heat. French bread, green salad, and red wine round out the meal admirably.

The number of eggs can be varied to suit your taste—and number of guests; the more you use, the more cohesive the mixture will be.

In the kitchen: Brown ground beef well in oil in a large frying pan over high heat.

Add onions, garlic, and mushrooms (if used) to the ground meat; reduce heat and continue cooking, stirring occasionally, until onion is soft. Bring to the table with seasonings, spinach and eggs; place over table top burner.

Stir in seasonings and spinach; cook for about 5 minutes longer. Add eggs; stir mixture over low heat just until eggs begin to set. Makes 4 to 6 servings.

CHAFING DISH ENTREES

Baked Meatballs and Variations

1½ pounds lean ground beef (preferably chuck or round)
⅓ cup milk
⅓ cup fine dry bread crumbs
2 teaspoons instant minced onion
2 eggs
1 teaspoon Worcestershire
¾ teaspoon salt
⅛ teaspoon pepper

For an easy dinner that can be prepared ahead of time, consider one of these fancy meatball dishes inspired by international classics. You mix and shape the basic meatballs and ready the selected sauce in advance. Both are then chilled. Shortly before announcing dinner, you quickly bake the meatballs, heat the sauce, and serve intriguingly—and effortlessly—from the chafing dish with rice or noodles.

In a bowl combine all ingredients. Mix together with your fingers until blended; shape into balls using about 2 tablespoons mixture for each. Place on a greased rimmed baking sheet, cover, and chill well.

When ready to bake, place cold meatballs in a 500° oven for about 12 minutes, or until just slightly pink inside. Serve in one of the following ways:

Meatballs in Wine Sauce

¼ cup butter or margarine
½ pound mushrooms, quartered
¾ cup water
1 teaspoon beef stock base or 1 beef bouillon cube
¾ cup dry red wine (Burgundy or Chianti)
2 tablespoons catsup
1 bay leaf
1 can (8 oz.) tiny whole onions, drained
1 clove garlic, minced or mashed
¼ cup cold water
4 teaspoons cornstarch
Cooked rice

In a chafing dish, melt butter; add mushrooms and stir over medium heat until mushrooms are golden. Pour in the ¾ cup water, sprinkle in beef stock or bouillon cube, and stir to dissolve. Then add wine, catsup, bay leaf, onions, and garlic. Slowly blend ¼ cup cold water into cornstarch; gradually stir into pan. Cook, stirring, until mixture boils and thickens. Cover and chill if made ahead.

To serve, prepare enough rice for 4 servings according to package directions. Bake meatballs as directed. Reheat sauce in chafing dish, add meatballs, and heat thoroughly, stirring often. Arrange the rice on a heated serving platter or place in a bowl. Bring to the table with the meatballs and sauce, placing the chafing dish over a low flame or use the bain-marie to prevent scorching. Makes 4 servings.

Meatballs with Curry Sauce

¼ cup salad oil
1 medium-sized onion, sliced
1 teaspoon curry powder
1 teaspoon ground coriander
1 clove garlic, minced or mashed
1 stick whole cinnamon
6 whole cloves
½ teaspoon ground cumin
½ cup milk
2 teaspoons cornstarch
1 cup unflavored yogurt
Cooked rice

In a chafing dish, heat salad oil; add onion, curry, coriander, garlic, cinnamon, cloves, and cumin. Stir until onions are limp and translucent. Slowly blend milk into cornstarch until smooth; then stir into onion mixture with yogurt. Heat, stirring, until mixture boils and thickens. Discard the cloves, cover, and chill (if made ahead).

To serve, prepare rice for 4 servings according to package directions. Bake meatballs as directed. Reheat sauce in chafing dish, add meatballs, and heat thoroughly, stirring often. Arrange the rice on a heated serving platter or place in a bowl. Bring to the table with the meatballs and sauce, placing the chafing dish over low flame or over a water pan to keep warm. Makes 4 servings.

Meatballs Sauerbraten

¼ cup butter or margarine
1 medium-sized onion, sliced
2 medium-sized carrots, sliced thinly on the diagonal
1 bay leaf
2 tablespoons brown sugar
1 can (14 oz.) regular-strength beef broth
6 tablespoons lemon juice
¼ cup raisins
⅛ teaspoon ground ginger
¼ cup cold water
5 teaspoons cornstarch
Cooked egg noodles

In a chafing dish, melt butter; add onion, carrots, and bay leaf; stir until onions are limp and translucent. Then stir in brown sugar, beef broth, lemon juice, raisins, and ground ginger. Slowly blend cold water into cornstarch; gradually stir into pan. Cook, stirring constantly, until mixture boils and thickens. Cover and chill if made ahead.

To serve, prepare egg noodles for 4 servings according to package directions. Bake meatballs as directed. Reheat sauce in chafing dish and add meatballs. Arrange the noodles on a heated serving platter or place in a bowl. Bring to the table with the meatballs and sauce, placing the chafing dish over low flame or use the bain-marie to prevent scorching. Makes 4 servings.

Swiss Julienne of Veal (Geschnetzeltes)

2 pounds boneless veal cutlets, ⅓ inch thick
Salt
Pepper
Paprika
3 tablespoons butter or margarine
2 tablespoons chopped shallots or green onions
3 tablespoons flour
1 cup whipping cream
½ cup dry white wine
¼ cup brandy or cognac

Swiss julienne of veal, geschnetzeltes, is offered on restaurant menus throughout Switzerland. It is a simple combination of quickly-cooked julienne strips of veal in a rich wine-accented sauce. The make-ahead character of this dish makes it ideally suited to company entertaining since preliminary mess is out of the way and all that's left is the finishing touch—which is done with finesse at the table.

To complete the meal we suggest the traditional accompaniment, "rösti" potatoes (diced, buttery, pan-roasted potatoes), a crisp green salad, and hard rolls.

Carefully trim away skin or fat from veal. Put one piece at a time between two pieces of waxed paper and pound with a smooth-surfaced mallet to flatten it evenly to about ¼ inch thickness. Sprinkle meat lightly on each side with salt, pepper, and paprika.

Cut into strips ¼ inch wide and about 1½ inches long.

In a wide frying pan over the range, heat butter until bubbly. Add shallots or onions and sauté until just softened.

Add veal strips and cook over medium-high heat, stirring frequently, until no longer pink, about 4 minutes. Remove meat and shallots or onion to a 1-quart bowl.

Stir flour into drippings in pan; cook, stirring, until bubbly. Gradually blend in whipping cream and wine. Cook, stirring, until thickened and smooth. (If you plan to serve this dish later, cover and refrigerate the meat and the sauce separately.)

Shortly before serving, add cooked meat to hot (or reheated) sauce in a chafing dish or other pan. Cook, stirring frequently, about 5 minutes or until heated through.

Heat brandy in a small pan; ignite, and pour over veal in sauce. Stir until flames die down, then serve. Makes about 6 servings.

CHAFING DISH ENTREES

Scallopini Picatte

*2 boned veal round steaks
(about 1 lb.), skin removed
Flour
4 tablespoons (⅛ lb.) butter
Salt and pepper
Juice of 1 lemon (about 3 tablespoons)
Lemon wedges*

This quick sauté dish is one of the many lesser known versions of scallopini that fine Italian restaurants sometimes have on their menus. It is simply veal steak pounded paper thin, dusted with flour, browned in butter, and served with the juice of a lemon squeezed over the meat.

For your table top performance, bring on the ingredients following the flouring of the veal. The pan should be well heated so meat browns and cooks quickly.

Place veal between waxed paper and pound with a flat wooden mallet until about ¼ inch thick. Cut into serving size pieces and coat with flour, shaking off the excess.

Heat butter in a wide frying pan over direct high heat until sizzling. Add veal without crowding and brown quickly (about 30 seconds) on each side. Place on a hot serving tray, pour pan drippings over meat, sprinkle with salt and pepper and the squeezed lemon juice. Garnish with lemon wedges. Serve at once. Makes 4 servings.

Fettucine

*3 cups hot boiled fettucine,
tagliarini or egg noodles (packaged
or freshly made)
Hot water
6 tablespoons butter
1¼ cups heavy cream
1 cup shredded Parmesan cheese
Salt and pepper
Fresh grated nutmeg
(or ground nutmeg)*

A delicious pasta dish, drenched in a creamy cheese sauce which you blend in just before serving, is an ideal choice for a late-night supper party with an Italian accent.

With it, you might serve an antipasto platter laden with canned albacore tuna mounded or left in a round chunk, pitted ripe olives, marinated artichoke hearts, celery sticks, cherry tomatoes, canned pickled red hot chiles, and thin-sliced salami; bread sticks and well-browned Italian sausages are good flavor and texture complements.

Light but thorough tossing is the secret. Pasta should be neither dry nor soupy. For a nice touch, dust a little Parmesan over each plate just prior to serving this delicately-flavored appetizer-entree.

Keep the noodles warm after cooking by floating in water that is hot to touch. In a wide frying pan or chafing dish over high heat on a range, melt butter until it is lightly browned. Add ½ cup of the cream and boil rapidly until large shiny bubbles form; stir occasionally. (You can make this part of the sauce earlier in the day, then reheat.)

At the table: Reduce heat to medium or place chafing dish over direct flame. Drain noodles well and add to the sauce. Toss vigorously with 2 forks, and pour in the cheese and the remaining cream, a little at a time—about three additions. The noodles should be kept moist but not too liquid. Season with salt and pepper and grate nutmeg generously over the noodles (or use about ⅛ teaspoon of the ground spice). Serve immediately. Makes 4 generous or 6 ample servings.

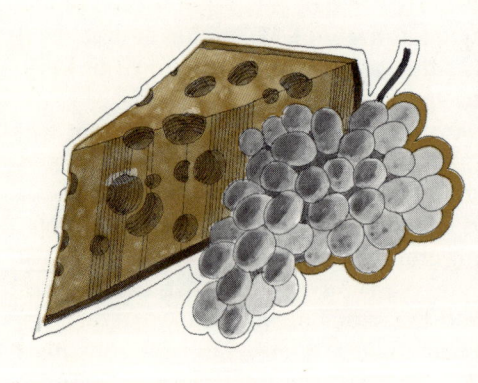

CHAFING DISH ENTREES

Glazed Breast of Chicken With Grapes

4 whole chicken breasts (about 3½ pounds), split, boned, and skin removed
½ cup flour
½ teaspoon salt
¼ teaspoon nutmeg
6 tablespoons melted butter or margarine
2 cups seedless grapes, washed and drained
2 tablespoons orange marmalade
Small bunches of grapes

Combine nutmeg-spiced chicken breast strips with glazed grapes for a superb brunch offering. The chicken cooks quickly over medium flame, making it possible to prepare this entree completely at the table.

Serve with iced tomato juice, toasted English muffins or sourdough bread, and plenty of freshly-brewed coffee.

Cut chicken meat lengthwise in strips about ½ inch wide. Dust with a mixture of flour, salt, and nutmeg. Shake off excess.

At the table: In a large frying pan over a portable burner (or in an electric skillet set at 300°), lightly brown strips of chicken in melted butter or margarine. Push strips to one side.

Add grapes; stir to heat through. Gently mix grapes and chicken with orange marmalade.

Turn flame down so chicken stays warm. Serve from pan. Garnish each plate with a small bunch of grapes. Makes 4 to 6 servings.

Cashew Chicken

3 whole chicken breasts, boned, and skin removed
½ pound Chinese (edible pod) peas or 1 package (10 oz.) frozen pod peas, partially thawed
½ pound mushrooms
4 green onions
1 can (15 oz.) bamboo shoots, drained
1 tablespoon chicken stock base dissolved in 1 cup water, or 1 cup regular-strength chicken broth
¼ cup soy sauce
2 tablespoons cornstarch
½ teaspoon sugar
½ teaspoon salt
¼ cup salad oil
1 package (4 oz.) cashews

Despite the lengthy grocery list, preliminary planning and proper heat are all this dish requires. Arrange all the ingredients on trays to take to the table for cooking, which is completed within 5 minutes. Direct high heat is necessary for best results.

Slice chicken breasts horizontally in ⅛-inch slices, then cut in 1-inch squares. Arrange on a tray.

Remove the ends and strings from fresh peas. Wash and slice mushrooms. Cut the green part of the onions into 1-inch lengths and then slash both ends several times making small fans; slice the white part ¼ inch thick. Slice bamboo shoots.

Arrange all the vegetables on a tray.

Pour chicken broth into a small pitcher. Mix together soy sauce, cornstarch, sugar, and salt; pour into a small pitcher. Place oil and cashews in separate small containers. Arrange at the table with alcohol or canned heat table top burner (or use an electric frying pan).

To cook, heat frying pan (or electric frying pan to 350°); add 1 tablespoon of the oil, then add nuts all at once and cook over moderate heat 1 minute, shaking pan, until nuts are lightly toasted. Remove from pan and set aside.

Add remaining oil to pan; add chicken, and cook quickly, turning until it turns opaque. Add peas and mushrooms. Pour in broth, cover, and simmer 2 minutes.

Add bamboo shoots. Stir the soy sauce mixture into the pan juices, and cook until sauce is thickened, stirring constantly; then simmer 1 minute uncovered. Mix in the green onions. Sprinkle with nuts. Makes 6 servings.

CHAFING DISH ENTREES

Chicken Normandy
(Poulet à la Vallée d'Auge)

1 large roasting chicken (about 5½ lbs.), or a large broiler-fryer (3¾ to 4 lbs.), cut up
Salt and white pepper
3 tablespoons butter or margarine
5 shallots, finely chopped, or the white part of 6 large green onions, thinly sliced
½ cup Calvados, apple brandy, applejack, or brandy
¼ teaspoon whole thyme
½ cup apple juice
½ cup whipping cream
2 egg yolks, slightly beaten
Drained spiced crab apples (optional)
Parsley

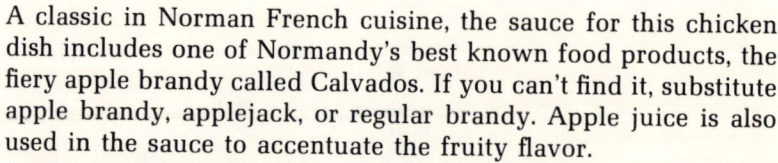

A classic in Norman French cuisine, the sauce for this chicken dish includes one of Normandy's best known food products, the fiery apple brandy called Calvados. If you can't find it, substitute apple brandy, applejack, or regular brandy. Apple juice is also used in the sauce to accentuate the fruity flavor.

The chicken is flamed twice—once in the kitchen before it is completely cooked, then again at the table. For this second application, ladle on the flaming brandy a spoonful at a time to prolong the pyrotechnics.

If you prefer, you can partially cook the chicken ahead of time. Return it to the oven until it is tender and heated through, then prepare the sauce. Serve it with thin French-fried potatoes or steamed rice, and fresh or frozen asparagus.

Sprinkle chicken pieces lightly with salt and pepper. Brown well on all sides in butter in a large frying pan over medium-high heat; as pieces brown, remove to a large casserole or Dutch oven.

Remove pan from heat, add shallots, and let cook until soft; remove from pan with slotted spoon and distribute over chicken. Discard pan drippings.

Add ¼ cup of the Calvados to the warm pan; ignite it and let burn, tipping pan back and forth gently, until flames dissipate.

Stir in thyme and apple juice, scraping brown particles from pan bottom. Pour over chicken, cover, and place in a 350° oven for about 1 hour (about 45 minutes for a broiler-fryer) or until chicken is tender. Remove chicken to a warm serving dish.

Add cream to cooking liquid. Cook quickly to reduce liquid to about 1½ cups; stir a little of the hot liquid into egg yolks. Return egg mixture to pan and cook, stirring constantly, over medium heat just until thickened (do not boil).

Pour sauce over chicken; garnish with crab apples and parsley.

At the table heat remaining ¼ cup of Calvados in a small pan, ignite, and pour over chicken. Makes 6 servings, or 5 from a broiler-fryer.

Chicken Livers in Cream

¼ cup butter
1 pound chicken livers, halved
1 tablespoon minced shallots or green onions
Salt and pepper
2 tablespoons cognac
1 cup heavy cream
Very finely minced parsley
Toast

This is an excellent choice for a party brunch. Chicken liver lovers will approve heartily.

Heat butter in a chafing dish or frying pan. Add chicken livers and shallots or green onions and sauté over direct high flame. When lightly browned, sprinkle with salt and pepper. Pour cognac over; heat quickly, light and allow the flames to die out.

Add cream and cook quickly until cream is reduced about ⅓. Sprinkle with parsley; serve on toast. Makes 4 to 6 servings.

CHAFING DISH ENTREES

Chicken Breasts Mère Catherine

4 whole chicken breasts, split, boned, and skin removed
Salt to taste
3 tablespoons butter
⅓ cup brandy
¼ cup dry red wine
Béarnaise Sauce (recipe follows)
Chopped parsley

Although flaming brandy is important in creating the sauce for this dish, it is added midway in preparation, instead of just before serving.

Have all elements ready before you begin to cook. Cook the chicken first in the kitchen so spattering is kept from the dining room. Béarnaise may be prepared while the chicken sizzles, but should be kept warm if not used immediately.

To complete the menu, serve sautéed vegetables, rice (perfect with the extra sauce), and oil-and-vinegar-dressed butter lettuce or romaine. Dessert might be a smooth fondue sauce with a selection of fresh fruits.

Sprinkle chicken lightly with salt; brown lightly in butter on both sides over medium-high heat in blazer pan of chafing dish (or in frying pan over a portable burner). Cover and cook slowly for about 10 to 15 minutes, depending upon meatiness, just until chicken is cooked through. Remove chicken from pan. Keep warm in oven or on hot tray.

At the table, add brandy to warm pan; place over flame. Ignite and let it burn, tipping pan from side to side, until flames are gone. Stir in red wine and cook quickly to reduce liquid slightly, stirring occasionally.

Turn off heat and blend in Béarnaise (recipe follows) until smooth. Return chicken to pan, turning to coat with sauce. Sprinkle with chopped parsley. Serve immediately. Makes 4 generous servings.

Béarnaise Sauce

1 egg
1 teaspoon tarragon vinegar
1 teaspoon Dijon-style mustard
1 tablespoon lemon juice
½ cup warm, melted butter

Place in blender container egg, vinegar, mustard, and lemon juice. Blend for a few seconds, then with motor running, slowly pour in butter, blending until thickened.

Keep warm in top of double boiler over hot water until ready to use; or make ahead and reheat slowly in double boiler over barely simmering water, stirring occasionally, until smooth. Makes about ¾ cup.

CHAFING DISH ENTREES

Chicken in Casserole With Grapes

12 pieces of chicken (breasts, thighs, drumsticks, or any combination)
Salt and pepper
Flour
5 tablespoons butter or margarine
¼ cup minced onion
¼ cup chicken broth
¾ cup dry white table wine
½ pound mushrooms, sliced
3 tablespoons butter or margarine
2 cups seeded Muscat grapes or Thompson seedless grapes

Green grapes and sautéed sliced mushrooms are the finishing touches for this delicately seasoned chicken baked in a light wine sauce. Although all cooking is first done in a frying pan and then in the oven, this entree will hold for up to an hour in your chafing dish.

Sprinkle chicken pieces with salt and pepper and coat lightly with flour. Heat the 5 tablespoons butter in a frying pan and quickly brown chicken on all sides.

Arrange pieces closely together in a single layer in a large shallow baking pan.

Add onion to butter in frying pan; cook until soft. Add chicken broth and wine; bring to a boil, then pour over chicken. Bake, covered, in a 375° oven for 40 minutes.

Meanwhile, sauté mushrooms in the 3 tablespoons butter. When chicken has cooked for 40 minutes, add the mushrooms and grapes; continue baking, covered, for 8 minutes more, or until grapes are just heated.

Arrange on a platter or serve from a chafing dish. Makes 6 to 8 servings.

Salmon Fillets Flambé

2½ pounds (approximately) whole salmon fillet or a center chunk boned and filleted
Lemon Basting Sauce (recipe follows)
3 tablespoons butter
⅓ cup finely minced parsley
2 green onions, finely chopped
1 teaspoon whole tarragon
2 tablespoons Calvados, apple brandy, or Pernod

The showmanship enters at the end—with the drama of flaming brandy spooned over broiled salmon fillets.

Place salmon skin side up on broiler rack; brush with Lemon Basting Sauce, and place about 5 inches under preheated broiler. Broil about 20 to 25 minutes, *not* turning, until fish flakes easily when tested with a fork.

Meanwhile, melt butter in a large, flameproof serving dish or frying pan; with a spatula transfer the cooked fish to the dish or pan. Combine the parsley, onions, and tarragon and sprinkle in a ribbon down the fish. Bring to the table. To flame, heat the Calvados, apple brandy, or Pernod in a small pan; ignite, and spoon flaming over the fish. Serves 8.

Lemon Basting Sauce

4 tablespoons (¼ cup) butter or margarine
3 tablespoons lemon juice
1 teaspoon salt
½ teaspoon whole tarragon
Dash of freshly ground pepper

In a small saucepan melt butter. Add other ingredients. Use to baste fish during cooking.

Almond-Sauced Scallops

¼ cup (⅛ lb.) butter or margarine
¾ cup sliced unblanched almonds
1½ pounds scallops
½ cup half-and-half
(half milk, half cream)
3 tablespoons finely chopped parsley
½ teaspoon salt
⅛ teaspoon oregano
Dash pepper
2 tablespoons dry Sherry
1 tablespoon cornstarch
1½ teaspoons lemon juice
Hot cooked rice

Scallops are an elegant main dish when done in a toasted almond sauce with an assortment of complementary seasonings. Serve over fluffy rice accompanied by whole green beans, flaky dinner rolls, and a dry white wine.

Melt butter in blazer pan of chafing dish over direct heat; add almonds, and cook until lightly browned.
    Stir in scallops; cook, stirring gently now and then, until scallops lose their translucent look.
    Blend in half-and-half, parsley, salt, oregano, and pepper. Blend Sherry smoothly with cornstarch; stir into scallops and cook, stirring occasionally, until thickened. Blend in lemon juice. Serve with rice. Makes 4 servings.

Shrimp and Mushroom Sauté

2 tablespoons butter
½ pound medium-sized mushrooms, sliced
⅓ cup dry Sherry or 2 tablespoons lemon juice
1½ pounds medium-sized raw shrimp, shelled and deveined
2 green onions, chopped
Sour cream (garnish)
Parsley (garnish)

This dish is ideal brunch fare, served perhaps with fresh fruit, French bread heated with cheese, and coffee.

Measure out all ingredients, place in bowls and bring to the table on a tray. Have chafing dish or frying pan preheated over kitchen range or table top heating unit. When pan is hot, add butter; then add mushrooms and sauté for about 3 minutes.
    Add Sherry or lemon juice and shrimp; cook over direct flame, turning, until shrimp become pink, about 5 minutes. Sprinkle with green onions. Garnish each serving with a small spoonful of sour cream and sprinkle with chopped parsley. Serves 4.

Crab-Filled Brunch Pancakes

1 cup prepared pancake mix
2 eggs
About 2¼ cups milk
About 4 tablespoons butter or margarine
2 tablespoons flour
½ teaspoon dry mustard
2 teaspoons anchovy paste
2 cups (about ¾ lb.) crab meat
2 tablespoons finely minced parsley
Salt and pepper to taste
1 avocado, seeded, peeled, sliced, and sprinkled with about 1 tablespoon lemon juice

For ease in assembling and serving, the pancakes could be baked on an electric griddle or frying pan at the table; the crab filling is kept hot in a chafing dish or fondue pot.

In a bowl combine the pancake mix, eggs, and ¾ cup of the milk. Stir until well blended. Melt the butter in a frying pan, measure 2 tablespoons of the butter, and stir into pancake batter; set aside.
    Blend flour and mustard into remaining butter in pan and cook, stirring, until bubbly. Gradually stir in remaining 1½ cups milk, then cook and stir until it boils and thickens.
    Remove from heat and mix in the anchovy paste, crab meat, parsley, and salt and pepper to taste. Transfer to a chafing dish, fondue pot, or similar dish and keep warm.
    Bake pancakes on a hot, lightly greased griddle. Serve with warm crab filling and top with avocado. Makes about 6 servings.

CHAFING DISH ENTREES

Fresh fruits are dipped in a simple but rich dessert fondue sauce (pages 74–75) for a flavorful finale.

66 DESSERTS... PREPARED AT THE TABLE

Desserts... Prepared at the Table

In this chapter you will find a variety of fruit desserts, fondue and other sauces, basic crêpes and newly-created variations, and airy zabaglione.

With few exceptions, all are easily prepared. Many are completely prepared ahead and then merely heated or, more likely, dramatically flamed at the table; some are as simple as sauces for spooning over ice cream. A few require more expertise and showmanship, but will be easy to prepare once you have mastered the techniques in the simpler recipes.

As far as equipment is concerned, the desserts category contains the most adaptable recipes suitable for cooking at the table. Often, either classic chafing dish or standard metal fondue pot are interchangeable. The only definite exceptions seem to be crêpes, which require a larger, shallow surface, and some sauces, which are served in smaller dishes and remain warm with the aid of a candle or trivet after initial heating has been completed in the kitchen.

Detailed directions for flaming foods are on page 8, since this information can apply to every type of food and course.

Surprisingly, many of these desserts are ideal when you have last-minute guests; a fair number of the recipes are made from ingredients that are considered by many cooks to be "pantry staples" . . . spices, butter, fruits, liqueurs, nuts, ice cream.

Whether you're young, older, single or married, male or female, these recipes can provide an interesting change of pace from what is probably your normal routine. Practically any get-together with friends calls for food; it just seems natural. To present it uniquely, bring out your chafing dish and tray—or suitable substitute—with all the ingredients measured, place in front of your guests, and assemble a dessert with ease. Of course it's a good idea if you've practiced preceding this performance, and for reassurance it's wise to tuck a copy of the recipe discreetly in a corner of the tray.

The common denominator within this chapter: A finale with a flourish, even something simple, adds a lot of interest to any dinner party or dessert occasion.

Flaming Dessert Bananas

2 or 3 medium-ripe bananas
½ teaspoon grated orange peel
3 tablespoons butter
2 tablespoons sugar
¼ cup Cointreau (or other orange-flavored liqueur)
Sweetened whipped cream

An accent of orange makes a pleasant contrast to mild-flavored bananas. A topping of whipped cream gilds the combination.

Peel bananas, cut in half lengthwise and then crosswise; put in a dish and sprinkle with orange peel. Bring to the table with butter, sugar, liqueur in a long-handled pan, whipped cream.

At the table melt butter in a chafing dish over direct flame. Add bananas, cut side up. Cook quickly until lightly browned; turn cut sides down into butter.

Sprinkle with sugar. Simmer until fruit is browned on all sides. Heat the liqueur, ignite, and pour over the bananas and stir until flames die down. Serve fruit in bowls, top with spoonfuls of sweetened whipped cream, and then drizzle with sauce from bananas. Makes about 4 servings.

Cherries Jubilee

1 can (1 lb.) pitted dark sweet cherries
1 tablespoon cornstarch
2 tablespoons sugar
Dash each salt and cinnamon
1 tablespoon lemon juice
¼ cup brandy
Vanilla ice cream

This version is designed for two. If you wish, prepare it at the table; if you're timid, just flame it at the table. Either way, he'll know you can cook.

Drain cherries, saving ½ cup of the syrup. In chafing dish, fondue pot, or saucepan, combine cornstarch, the reserved syrup, sugar, salt, and cinnamon.

In the kitchen, or at the table, bring to a boil over direct heat; stir and cook until liquid is clear and thickened.

Remove from heat and stir in lemon juice and cherries.

If you prepare sauce in the kitchen, reheat at the table.

In a small, long-handled pan, heat the brandy; ignite; pour over fruit, stirring. Spoon flaming fruit and sauce over individual servings of ice cream. Makes 2 generous servings.

Chafing Dish Apples

2 large cooking apples (Golden Delicious or Winesap)
¼ cup butter or margarine
¼ cup brown sugar
¼ cup rum

Rum flames and flavors this apple dessert. After the flames subside, serve alone, or you could spoon it over ice cream.

Peel, core, and slice the apples. Place chafing dish or an attractive frying pan over medium heat on your kitchen range. Melt butter, stir in sugar; then add apples; glaze on both sides, about 10 minutes.

Bring to the table and place over low heat. Heat rum in a small pan, ignite, and pour over apples; stir until flames die. Makes about 4 servings.

DESSERTS...PREPARED AT THE TABLE

Strawberries Fire and Ice

About 1 quart vanilla ice cream
About 2½ cups strawberries
¼ cup sugar
1 tablespoon cornstarch
⅓ cup orange juice
3 tablespoons Cointreau or other orange-flavored liqueur
Sweetened whipped cream (optional)

Ice cream balls are prepared in advance; assembly and actual cooking are completed in minutes. For a variation, try also the peaches-and-brandy combination.

At least 2 hours in advance, place 8 scoops ice cream on a baking sheet (or in 4 dessert bowls that can withstand change of temperature from freezer to heat of sauce); freeze until solid.

Wash, hull, and halve strawberries; set aside.

In a chafing dish or fondue pot mix together sugar and cornstarch to blend; stir in the orange juice, a little at a time, until smooth. Place chafing dish directly over medium heat of range (chafing dish flame is usually too slow); stir constantly until mixture boils and thickens; set aside.

For table presentation: Assemble on a tray the chafing dish with cooked cornstarch mixture, 4 serving dishes filled with 2 scoops of ice cream each, orange-flavored liqueur in a small long-handled pan, the strawberries, and whipped cream.

At the table heat cornstarch mixture over direct flame until bubbles form; then add strawberries, stirring gently but thoroughly.

Heat the liqueur, ignite, and pour into chafing dish; stir until flames die down. Spoon mixture over ice cream in dishes. Serve immediately, with whipped cream, if desired. Makes 4 servings.

Peaches Fire and Ice: Substitute 2½ cups fresh peeled, sliced peaches mixed with 1 tablespoon lemon juice, or 2½ cups canned, sliced peaches, in place of the berries. Use brandy instead of orange-flavored liqueur.

Stuffed Figs in Wine Sauce

1 package (1 lb.) dried Calimyrna figs
¾ cup shredded medium sharp Cheddar cheese
¾ cup finely chopped pecans
½ cup sugar
1 tablespoon cornstarch
1½ cups Sauterne
3 tablespoons butter
¼ teaspoon grated orange peel
Shredded Cheddar cheese (optional)

Figs become plump and flavorful after a slow simmering in a Sauterne sauce; it's mostly done ahead, ready to finish cooking at the table.

The surprise inside the figs is a mixture of shredded Cheddar and chopped pecans. Essence of orange peel flatters fruit, cheese, and wine.

Cut stem from each fig; through top opening fill with a mixture of cheese and nuts.

In the kitchen, combine sugar and cornstarch in the chafing dish; stir in 1 cup of the wine. Cook, stirring, over high heat until sauce is thick and clear.

Add butter, orange peel, remaining wine, and figs. Remove from heat. This much can be done ahead.

At the table, heat figs in sauce to simmering, stirring and basting figs with sauce occasionally, until heated through and figs are slightly plumped. Serve with some of the sauce spooned over figs; top with a sprinkling of cheese. Makes 8 to 10 servings.

DESSERTS... PREPARED AT THE TABLE

Peaches and Rum Babas

1 can (12 oz.) rum baba cakes (4 cakes)
2 large peaches or nectarines, peeled and halved
¼ cup almond macaroon cooky crumbs
2 tablespoons soft butter
3 tablespoons rum

The showiness of presentation belies the simplicity of preparation. Canned rum baba cakes are the base for this dessert. Fresh peaches or nectarines go atop each cake; flaming rum is the finishing touch done at the table.

Arrange the rum baba cakes in a greased shallow baking pan or ovenproof serving plate, pouring over any syrup from the can. Arrange a peach half, with cut side up, on top of each rum cake.

Combine cooky crumbs with butter to make a paste; spoon on the peach halves. Bake, uncovered, in a 350° oven for about 30 minutes. Bring warm to the table.

Heat the rum in a small container over a candle or other warmer at the table; ignite it, and pour over the warm peaches. Makes 4 servings.

Ice Cream Mold with Flaming Nut Sauce

½ gallon coffee ice cream
2 tablespoons butter
¾ cup coarsely chopped Brazil nuts
¼ cup brandy

A handsome coffee ice cream mold is handy to have on hand when the occasion calls for an impressive dessert finale. The base is made in advance and waits in the freezer; the flaming sauce is added in front of guests.

Let ice cream soften slightly; pack into a fancy 2-quart mold, cover with foil, and return to the freezer for at least 2 hours, or until solidly frozen. Dip mold in lukewarm water for a few seconds, then turn upside down on a large serving plate. Return to the freezer until needed.

At the table in a small pan over direct flame, melt butter; add nuts and brown them lightly. In another small pan, heat the brandy, ignite, and pour over the sauce. Spoon the flaming sauce over the ice cream. Serve at once. Makes 10 servings.

Hot Caramel Peaches

1 large can (about 1 lb. 14 oz.) cling peach halves
About ¼ cup brown sugar
¾ cup sour cream
Cinnamon

An easy recipe for the beginning performer. You simply heat the peaches before your audience, then serve with brown sugar and a cold dollop of sour cream.

Turn the peach halves and their syrup into your chafing dish. Stir over direct heat until the peaches are heated through.

To serve, place hot peach halves in small dessert dishes and top each with about 2 teaspoons brown sugar and about 2 tablespoons sour cream. Sprinkle with cinnamon. Makes 6 servings.

Butter Rum Figs

2 cups coarsely crumbled macaroon cookies
¾ teaspoon grated orange peel
¼ cup orange juice
⅔ cup light rum
About ½ gallon vanilla ice cream
¼ cup butter
¾ cup sugar
4 cups Mission or Kadota figs, cut in halves (peeled if desired) or 2 cans (about 16 oz. each) whole Kadota figs, drained

This partially-done-ahead-and-frozen dessert features figs in a butter sauce flavored with orange, flamed with rum. The base is a parfaitlike mixture of ice cream layered with cooky crumbs.

Mix together cooky crumbs, ½ teaspoon of the grated orange peel, orange juice, and ¼ cup of the rum. In a large chilled bowl or individual bowls, layer ice cream with the cooky mixture until all is used. Cover and freeze.

In a crêpes pan, frying pan, or chafing dish over direct flame, melt the butter; add sugar. Cook, stirring, just until sugar loses its grainy appearance and sauce is smooth.

Add remaining ¼ teaspoon orange peel and the figs. Turn fruit quickly to coat with sauce; figs should be heated but not cooked.

Warm remaining rum and pour, flaming, over the fruit. Spoon sauce over figs as it flames. Ladle fruit and sauce immediately over servings of the cooky-ice cream mixture. Makes 8 to 10 servings.

Praline Sundae Sauce

1 tablespoon butter
¾ cup coarsely chopped pecans
½ cup whipping cream
½ cup brown sugar, firmly packed
Vanilla or coffee ice cream

Hot pecan sauce served over vanilla or coffee ice cream makes a superb ending to a lighter meal. Ice cream is ready ahead and waiting in the freezer while this quick-to-fix sauce is stirred up. The heady aroma of heating butter, brown sugar, and pecans is surpassed only by the end results: sinfully rich flavor.

Melt butter in a chafing dish or small frying pan over moderate flame. Add pecans; heat and stir until lightly toasted. Add whipping cream and brown sugar. Bring to a boil and simmer just until blended, stirring constantly.

Ladle hot sauce over ice cream. Makes 4 servings.

Peaches in Hot Melba Sauce

1 package (10 oz.) frozen raspberries, forced through a wire strainer
⅓ cup currant jelly
3 tablespoons butter
½ teaspoon almond extract
2 cans (1 lb. each) peach halves, drained
Vanilla ice cream
Slivered almonds

Settle back, sip coffee, and relax a bit following dinner. This gives the peaches time to take on the rich red of the Melba sauce in which they simmer.

In a chafing dish over highest heat combine raspberry purée, jelly, butter, and almond extract. When mixture is simmering, add peaches. Cook gently, basting for about 7 minutes or until peaches have taken on a deep red color. Spoon peaches and sauce over ice cream; sprinkle with almonds. Serves 6.

Bananas in Cardamom Cream

4 tablespoons butter
2 tablespoons sugar
⅛ teaspoon cardamom
4 medium-ripe bananas
Juice of ½ lemon
¼ cup whipping cream
Additional whipping cream, if desired
Pound cake slices (optional)

Bananas are sautéed, then glazed with cream just before serving. The distinctive flavor of cardamom transforms this tropical fruit into an exceptionally fine finale.

Melt butter in a chafing dish or wide frying pan over direct flame; stir in sugar and cardamom.

Peel bananas and cut in slices about 1 inch thick directly into pan. Cook quickly over high heat, shaking (or turning with a spatula) until lightly brown on all sides.

Squeeze lemon juice into pan. (Prevent seeds from falling into dessert by wrapping lemon with cheesecloth.) Add whipping cream. Bring to boiling, stirring carefully so as not to mash bananas, until sauce thickens slightly.

Serve the fruit hot, spooning into individual dessert dishes alone, or over small slices of pound cake. Pour additional whipping cream over each portion if desired. Makes 4 servings.

Honey-Chocolate Sundae Sauce

½ cup butter or margarine
2 tablespoons cornstarch
½ cup cocoa
1 cup honey
1 cup water
½ teaspoon salt
Scant 2 cups miniature marshmallows (or 12 regular marshmallows)

Anyone who likes chocolate will enjoy this rich and airy sauce. Sweetened with honey and fluffed with marshmallows, these ingredients stay creamy and smooth even after being poured over ice cream.

In metal fondue pot or medium saucepan, melt butter; remove from heat. Stir in cornstarch, which has been mixed with the cocoa, until blended. Pour in honey and water.

Heat, stirring constantly, until sauce comes to a boil and thickens. Remove from heat; add salt and marshmallows; stir until marshmallows are melted.

Place over table top heating element to keep warm. Serve over ice cream. Makes about 3 cups sauce.

Mandarin Oranges Flambé

1 can (11 oz.) mandarin oranges, undrained
1 to 2 tablespoons brown sugar
Dash of cinnamon
3 tablespoons curaçao (or other orange-flavored liqueur), or chartreuse

This combination goes together quite simply . . . with splendid results.

Place mandarin oranges with their syrup in a chafing dish. Add brown sugar and cinnamon. Bring to the table with the liqueur in a small, long-handled pan.

Place oranges over flame, and when they are warm, heat the liqueur, ignite, and slowly pour over oranges, stir until flames die. Serve in long-stemmed glasses. Makes 2 to 4 servings.

DESSERTS . . . PREPARED AT THE TABLE

Triple Fruit Flambé

2 tablespoons butter
3 tablespoons honey
1 stick whole cinnamon
2 cans (11 oz. each) mandarin oranges, drained
1 package (10 oz.) frozen pitted dark cherries, thawed and drained
1 cup halved, seeded grapes, or seedless grapes
¼ cup kirsch or brandy
Vanilla ice cream

Mandarin oranges, dark cherries, and grapes are combined and heated through with a cinnamon stick accent. Flame with kirsch or brandy and serve over ice cream.

Combine in a chafing dish the butter, honey, and cinnamon stick. Add oranges, cherries, and grapes. Bring to the table and place over flame until heated through.

Heat kirsch or brandy, ignite, and pour over fruits; stir until the flames die. Spoon fruits and sauce over ice cream. Makes 6 servings.

Zabaglione

8 egg yolks
3 to 4 tablespoons sugar
½ cup Dry Sauterne, Dry Semillon, Malvasia Bianca, Marsala, Madeira, or sweet Muscatel

Zabaglione is like a custard, wine thickened by egg yolks, but you whip the mixture with a wire whip as it cooks, incorporating tiny air bubbles. The mixture cooks quickly, in about 5 minutes, and you serve it immediately.

The standard serving container is a handsome stemmed wine glass filled brimmingly full with this light, delicate foam.

After extensive testing and taste-sampling, we selected five wines as favorites. The zabaglione you like best will very likely be made with the wine you like best; individual taste is your guide. The traditional European choice is either a dry white wine or Marsala, and some food authorities consider Madeira equally good. Two California wines that our taste-testers felt were qualified to join these are Malvasia Bianca, a sweet white wine, and sweet Muscatel.

In a round bottom pan or top of a double boiler, beat together egg yolks, 3 tablespoons of the sugar, and the wine. Place the round bottom pan over direct heat (gas, electric, or denatured alcohol flame), or set the double boiler over gently simmering water. Whip mixture constantly with wire whip until it is thick enough to retain briefly a slight peak when whip is withdrawn; it takes about 5 minutes, more or less.

Taste, and add the remaining sugar if desired. Pour into stemmed glasses (it is not hot enough to require preheating glasses) and serve at once. Serves 6 to 8.

Here are some flavor variations:

Zabaglione with Grenadine. Add ½ teaspoon vanilla to zabaglione made with Dry Sauterne, Dry Semillon, or Malvasia Bianca. Pour ½ inch chilled grenadine in the bottom of each serving glass, fill; dust each serving with nutmeg.

Sherry Zabaglione. Add 1 tablespoon Sherry to zabaglione made with Dry Sauterne or Dry Semillon.

Zabaglione with Cream. Spoon a little sweetened, ice-cold whipped cream into the bottom of each serving glass and top with any hot zabaglione.

Dessert Fondue Sauces

Rich dessert fondue is a delicious finale for informal meals when something sweet seems apropos.

The hostess simply prepares a small batch of sauce and serves it with a tray or platter of bite-sized bits of fruit, cookies, cake, and/or candies for dipping.

Only utensils needed are a small cocktail fork, regular fondue or salad fork, or sturdy bamboo skewer, and a dessert plate.

A special dessert fondue set is not essential for "proper" service; almost any small container will do. A flameproof dish—a cereal or soup bowl is usually the perfect size—may be placed atop the range over direct warm or low heat with no danger of scorching the sauce or cracking the dish. When the sauce is smooth, remove it to an electric trivet or set over a candle warmer.

Just remember to keep the heat low since these rich mixtures do have a tendency to scorch easily.

The following recipes provide the just-right touch to appease the sweet tooth. After trying these to get the feel, you'll probably enjoy experimenting on your own.

For dipping, allow approximately ½ to 1 cup of fruit for each serving, plus 3 or 4 split ladyfingers or 4 to 6 bite-sized cubes of cake. About 1 cup of sauce is sufficient for 6 servings. Sugar and cream, ideal with almost any fruit, form the base for four of the sauces. Each has a mildly defined flavor distinctly different from the others.

Powdered Sugar, Orange-Honey, and Butterscotch sauces seem to go best with well-ripened peaches, pineapple, bananas, seedless grapes, strawberries, raspberries, papayas, and mangoes; Burnt-Sugar Caramel complemented all these fruits except mild papaya.

Swiss Chocolate Fondue lays the foundation for a great many variations. For assured success, just remember to use a good-quality chocolate and be careful that it doesn't get too hot.

Powdered Sugar Fondue

1 cup unsifted powdered sugar
1 cup (½ pint) whipping cream
1 or 2 tablespoons kirsch or brandy to taste (optional)

In a small saucepan mix powdered sugar and whipping cream. Stirring, bring to a full, vigorously foaming boil; cook 30 seconds.

Pour into dessert fondue pot or other small dish; stir in brandy, if desired. Keep warm over very low heat. Makes about 1 cup sauce.

Butterscotch Fondue

1 cup (½ pint) whipping cream
½ cup firmly packed brown sugar
2 or 3 tablespoons rum, or to taste (optional)

In a small saucepan blend whipping cream and brown sugar. Stirring, bring to a full, vigorously foaming boil and cook about 30 seconds.

Pour into dessert fondue pot or other small dish and add rum to taste, if desired. Keep warm over very low heat. Makes about 1 cup sauce.

DESSERTS... PREPARED AT THE TABLE

Orange-Honey Fondue

¼ cup butter
½ cup whipping cream
2 tablespoons sugar
2 tablespoons honey
2 tablespoons orange marmalade
2 tablespoons orange-flavored liqueur

In a small saucepan combine butter, whipping cream, sugar, honey, and orange marmalade. Stirring, bring to a full, vigorously foaming boil; cook 30 seconds.

Pour into fondue pan, adding liqueur. Keep warm over very low heat. Makes about 1 cup or 4 to 6 servings.

Swiss Chocolate Fondue

12 ounces milk chocolate, semi-sweet baking chocolate, or other flavored chocolate
¾ cup whipping cream
3 tablespoons Cointreau, brandy, rum, or crème de menthe
2 medium-sized bananas
1½ cups strawberries
1½ cups fresh (or canned) pineapple cubes
6 slices angel food cake, about ¾ inch thick

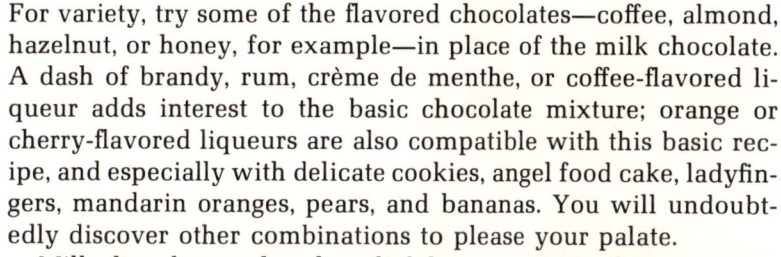

For variety, try some of the flavored chocolates—coffee, almond, hazelnut, or honey, for example—in place of the milk chocolate. A dash of brandy, rum, crème de menthe, or coffee-flavored liqueur adds interest to the basic chocolate mixture; orange or cherry-flavored liqueurs are also compatible with this basic recipe, and especially with delicate cookies, angel food cake, ladyfingers, mandarin oranges, pears, and bananas. You will undoubtedly discover other combinations to please your palate.

Milk chocolate, rather than dark bittersweet combinations, are usually preferred, since the dark chocolate can be overpowering. However, there is certainly no "rule"; it is a matter of taste.

Place chocolate and cream in the top of a double boiler; set over hot, not boiling, water and heat, stirring, until chocolate melts and blends with cream. Stir in liqueur or liquor.

Transfer to a small pan and place over a candle warmer or electric food warmer. (Be careful not to overheat chocolate sauce or it may scorch.)

Cut bananas into ½-inch sections and arrange on a tray with the hulled strawberries and pineapple cubes. Cut cake into bite-sized squares and add to the tray.

Place tray beside the hot chocolate sauce and accompany with bamboo skewers or fondue forks. Makes 6 to 8 servings.

Note: Any leftover sauce may be reheated and served over ice cream.

Burnt-Sugar Fondue

½ cup sugar
1 cup whipping cream

In a small saucepan over high heat cook ¼ cup of the sugar without stirring until it melts and caramelizes; tilt pan to mix.

At once pour in ½ cup of the whipping cream and cook over low heat, stirring frequently, until caramel dissolves.

Add the remaining ½ cup whipping cream and the remaining ¼ cup sugar. Stirring, bring to a full, vigorously foaming boil and cook about 30 seconds.

Pour into dessert fondue pot or other small dish and keep warm over very low heat. Makes about 1 cup sauce.

DESSERTS... PREPARED AT THE TABLE

French Crêpes

1 cup milk
3 eggs
⅔ cup regular all-purpose flour (unsifted)
About 4 teaspoons butter or margarine

These thin French crêpes can be made in advance and frozen or refrigerated until you are ready to use them. Stack the crêpes one atop another. When thoroughly cool, package airtight and refrigerate as long as a week, or freeze for longer storage. Thaw crêpes completely before separating.

You can make the crêpes in any small frying pan with a completely flat bottom so this thin batter will run freely to the edges and cook evenly. They are easiest to make in a special crêpe pan reserved for that task alone.

In a blender combine milk and eggs, then add flour. Cover and whirl smooth (or blend eggs and milk with a wire whip, then add flour and mix until smooth).

Place a 6 to 6½ inch crêpe pan (or other flat bottom frying pan of this dimension) on about medium heat. When the pan is hot, add ¼ teaspoon butter and swirl to coat surface. At once pour in about 1½ tablespoons of the batter, tilting pan so batter flows quickly over the entire flat surface.

If the heat is correct and the pan hot enough, the crêpe sets at once, forming tiny bubbles (don't worry if there are a few little holes); if the pan is too cool, the batter makes a smooth layer. Cook crêpe until the edge is lightly browned and the surface looks dry.

Because this crêpe tears easily, use this technique for turning it: Run a wide spatula around the edge to loosen in pan. Lay spatula on top of crêpe and invert with pan, turning the crêpe out onto the spatula. Then guide the crêpe, uncooked surface down, back into pan and brown lightly. Turn crêpe out of pan onto a plate.

Repeat this procedure to make each crêpe; stir batter occasionally and stack crêpes one atop another, If you do not use crêpes within a few hours, package airtight when cool and refrigerate as long as a week, or freeze for longer storage. Allow to warm throughout to room temperature before separating as they tear easily if cold. Makes about 16 crêpes.

Orange Crêpes

12 to 16 crêpes
4 tablespoons butter
6 tablespoons sugar
2 teaspoons grated orange peel
⅓ cup orange juice
¼ cup Cointreau (or other orange-flavored liqueur)
Fresh orange slices, optional

Fold crêpes in half, then in half again to form triangles.

In a wide frying pan or chafing dish over medium-high heat melt butter. Add sugar, orange peel, and orange juice; bring sauce to a full rolling boil.

Over an alcohol or canned heat flame (or on low heat) add folded crêpes to sauce, turning to coat surfaces. Set aflame heated Cointreau or other orange-flavored liqueur and pour over crêpes.

With a long handled spoon, ladle sauce over crêpes constantly until flame dies. Let simmer a few minutes, stirring gently as needed to prevent any scorching, then spoon crêpes and sauce onto serving dishes; allow 2 or 3 for a serving and accompany, if you like, with fresh orange slices. Makes 5 to 8 servings.

DESSERTS... PREPARED AT THE TABLE

Butter Cream Crêpes with Jam

4 tablespoons soft butter
1 cup unsifted powdered sugar
2 tablespoons rum or kirsch
16 crêpes
About ¾ cup jam (boysenberry or other tart berry jam is best with rum; apricot or cherry is best with kirsch)
4 tablespoons (¼ cup) rum or kirsch for flaming
Sweetened whipped cream, optional

Combine butter and sugar and beat until smoothly blended; then stir in 2 tablespoons rum or kirsch. Spread butter cream evenly over one side of each crêpe.

Then drizzle about 2 teaspoons jam down the center of each crêpe. Roll each crêpe around jam to form a slender cylinder. Place rolls, side by side and seam side down, in a shallow baking pan. Cover and chill until ready to serve; then bake, covered, in a 400° oven for 15 to 20 minutes, or until crêpes in center of pan are warmed.

At the table set rum or kirsch (corresponding to crêpe filling) aflame and pour over crêpes; with a long handled spoon, ladle juices in pan around crêpes continuously (to prevent edges from singeing) until flame dies. Serve crêpes, if desired, with sweetened whipped cream. Allow 2 or 3 crêpes for a serving. Makes 5 to 8 servings.

Crêpes Café Au Lait

12 crêpes
¼ cup firmly packed brown sugar
⅛ teaspoon cinnamon
½ cup whipping cream
6 tablespoons Kahlua or other coffee-flavored liqueur

Fold crêpes in half, then in half again to form triangles.

In a wide shallow frying pan or chafing dish combine brown sugar, cinnamon, and whipping cream. Bring to a full boil, stirring. Turn heat low or place over an alcohol or canned heat flame and add folded crêpes to pan, turning each to coat with sauce.

Set heated Kahlua aflame and pour over crêpes. With a long handled spoon ladle sauce continuously over crêpes until flame dies. Simmer several minutes and serve crêpes with sauce. Allow 2 crêpes for a serving. Makes 6 servings.

Ice Cream Crêpes with Flaming Blueberry Sauce

12 to 16 small balls of ice cream
12 to 16 crêpes
½ cup sugar
1 tablespoon cornstarch
½ cup water
1 package (10 oz.) frozen sugared blueberries
½ teaspoon grated lemon peel
2 teaspoons lemon juice
4 tablespoons (¼ cup) kirsch or rum

Place ice cream balls on a flat pan; freeze solid. Transfer to a bowl at serving time.

Fold each crêpe in half, then arrange them slightly overlapping in a shallow baking pan; cover. To heat, place, covered, in a 400° oven for about 8 minutes.

In a saucepan blend together sugar and cornstarch; gradually stir in water. Add blueberries, breaking apart, lemon peel, and lemon juice. Bring to a boil, stirring, and cook until sauce is thickened and clear.

Place sauce on low heat or over an alcohol or canned heat flame and assemble alongside the pan of hot crêpes and bowl of ice cream balls.

Set aflame heated kirsch or rum and pour into blueberry sauce; stir continuously until flame dies. For each serving, place a folded crêpe on a dish, top with 2 ice cream balls, another crêpe, then ladle on hot sauce. Makes 6 to 8 servings.

DESSERTS... PREPARED AT THE TABLE

Caramel Pear Crêpes

1 can (1 lb.) pears in heavy syrup, sliced
⅓ cup brown sugar, firmly packed
½ teaspoon grated lemon peel
1 small package (3 oz.) cream cheese
1 tablespoon brandy
1 tablespoon granulated sugar
⅓ cup sliced almonds
6 crêpes
¼ cup brandy (optional)

In the kitchen drain the syrup from the canned pears into a small saucepan; stir in the brown sugar and lemon peel, heat just until boiling and until the sugar is dissolved; reduce heat to keep warm.

Make the filling by combining in a small bowl the cream cheese, 1 tablespoon brandy, and granulated sugar; blend with a fork until smooth. Stir in almonds, reserving 1 tablespoon.

Carefully spread the crêpes with the cream cheese mixture to about ¾ inch from the edge. Place about 3 pear slices on one quarter of the crêpe with the ends coming to a point in the center and pointing out to the outer edge. Fold crêpe over them, forming a triangular case, and arrange in a chafing dish or electric frying pan; pour the heated sauce over top. Sprinkle with the remaining almond slices.

Bring to the table and set over a low flame or adjust heat to keep warm. Heat the brandy in a small pan, ignite, and pour over crêpes. Spoon sauce over crêpes until flame dies. Serve on small plates, spooning sauce over top. Makes 6 servings.

Strawberry Ice Cream Crêpes

Orange Sauce
16 crêpes, about 6 inches in diameter
1½ pints vanilla ice cream
4 cups strawberries, washed and halved
1 cup heavy cream, whipped and sweetened to taste (optional)
⅓ cup toasted sliced almonds (optional)

A fashionable Viennese restaurant, Cafe Franziskanerplatz, considers this dessert its house specialty. You can make the crêpes and orange sauce in advance and scoop and refreeze the ice cream ahead to simplify last-minute service. The whipped cream and almonds are optional.

To serve smoothly in front of guests, stack all the crêpes on one plate and dip them in the orange sauce, heated in a chafing dish or electric frying pan. Have the ice cream, whipped cream, strawberries, and nuts in bowls alongside so you can readily assemble each serving.

Depending on appetites, use 1 or 2 of the ice cream filled crêpes for each serving.

Prepare the orange sauce in the kitchen; if made ahead, reheat at the table. Place 6 tablespoons sugar in a small pan with a heavy bottom and heat over moderate heat, shaking the pan occasionally, until sugar melts and turns a light amber color (watch carefully so sugar does not scorch; shake or cover pan but do not stir).

Add 1 teaspoon slivered orange peel, 1 cup orange juice, 2 tablespoons lemon juice, and 3 tablespoons butter to caramelized sugar. Cover and simmer slowly just until sauce is blended together. Add 2 tablespoons orange-flavored liqueur.

Dip crêpes, one at a time, into hot orange sauce and place on dessert plate. Place 2 small spoonfuls of ice cream and some strawberries in the center of each crêpe.

Fold over two sides of the crêpe, making a neat roll, or rolls, on the dessert plate. Spoon over additional orange sauce. Then top with whipped cream and almonds, if used. Add a strawberry half for garnish. Repeat for each serving. Makes 8 or 16 servings.

DESSERTS... PREPARED AT THE TABLE

Brittany Crêpes with Ice Cream, Flambé

2 oz. semi-sweet chocolate
3 tablespoons butter or margarine
3 tablespoons powdered sugar
4 Brittany crêpes (recipe follows)
1 pint vanilla ice cream
3 tablespoons brandy (86 proof or higher)

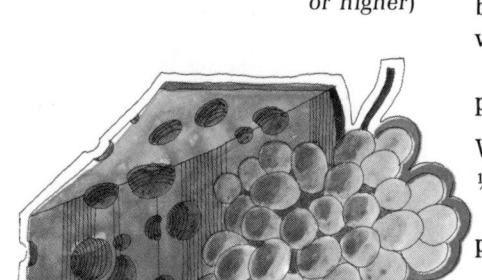

The crêpes are platter-sized. For this spectacular dessert, they are filled with ice cream and brought to the table in a good looking frying pan, heatproof serving platter, or chafing dish, then flamed.

While a special pan is traditionally used in France, these crêpes are not difficult to master using a standard frying pan with a bottom base that measures at least 8 or 10 inches across (pans with non-stick fluorocarbon finish are not recommended).

These big crêpes need to be cooked on one side only. At this point they freeze well. You can thaw and fill them anytime.

With a peeler, cut curls from chocolate (you should have about ⅓ cup).

Heat butter and sugar in a frying pan or other wide, shallow pan; set off heat.

Lay out crêpes, browned side down, and spoon a mound of ice cream in each. Fold crêpe over, envelope style; then quickly turn filled crêpes over in butter mixture and place seam side down in the pan. Sprinkle with chocolate curls and bring to the table.

Heat the brandy in a small pan in the kitchen or over flame at the table. Ignite brandy and pour over the crêpes. Serve on dessert plates. Makes 4 servings.

Brittany Crêpes

3 eggs
1½ cups milk
1 cup regular all-purpose flour (unsifted)
½ teaspoon salt
Butter

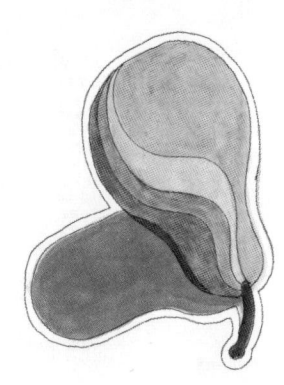

For the batter, combine the eggs, milk, flour, and salt in the blender container. Blend 30 seconds, clean blender sides, then blend about 1 minute more.

Cover and chill 30 minutes or longer. (Without a blender, beat the ingredients together until smooth, then chill.)

Place the frying pan over medium-high heat. Add about 2 teaspoons butter and tilt pan to coat.

Measure about ¼ cup batter for pan with 8-inch base or ⅓ cup batter for a 10-inch base pan. Lift the hot pan off heat, pour batter into pan, and immediately tip and tilt pan to coat bottom evenly.

Return pan to heat and cook a few seconds until edges are golden brown. Loosen edges with spatula, then flip pan over to turn crêpe out onto a baking sheet. Repeat, using all the batter and stacking crêpes as you work.

Index

Aïoli, 18-19
Ajoqueso, 13
Alcohol burners, 6, 7
Almond-Sauced Scallops, 65
Anchovy Sauce, 39
Appetizer Meatballs, 20
Appetizer Pancakes, 20-21
Appetizers, 10-21
Apples
  Chafing Dish, 68
  and Pears with
    Smoked Cheese Dip, 19
Avocado
  Curried Eggs with, 51
  Sauce, 41

Bagna Cauda, 14-15
Baked Meatballs, 58-59
Bananas
  in Cardamom Cream, 72
  Flaming Dessert, 68
Béarnaise Sauce
  Blender, 38
  for chicken breasts, 63
  Cold Blender, 38
  Mock, 38
Beef
  Dipping Kettle, 17
  Joe's Special, 57
  Meatballs, 20, 21, 58-59
  Medallions Sauté with
    Wild Rice, 56
  Steak Au Poivre, 56
  Steak Diane, 57
Blender
  Béarnaise Sauce, 38
  Curry Mayonnaise, 40
  Hollandaise Sauce, 40
Brittany Crêpes, 79
  with Ice Cream, Flambé, 79
Broth Fondue, 33-35
Brunch Swiss Fondue, 26
Bruncheon Mushrooms, 55
Burners, 6, 7
Burnt-Sugar Fondue, 75
Butane burners, 6, 7
Butter
  to clarify, 29
  Cream Crêpes with Jam, 77
  Herb, for cherry tomatoes
    and shrimp, 17
  Pesto, 44
  Rum Fig, 71
Buttermilk Cheese Dipping
  Sauce, 26
Butters, Flavored, 43
Butterscotch Fondue, 74

Candle heating units, 6
Canned heat burners, 6, 7
Caramel Pear Crêpes, 78
Cashew
  Chicken, 61
  Mushroom Medley, 54
Chafing Dish, 7, 46-65
  Apples, 68
Cheese
  Dip, Green Chile and, 12
  Dip, smoked, for apples
    and pears, 19
  Fondue, 24-27
  Fondue, Salami and, 13;
    photograph, 10
Cherries
  Jubilee, 68
  in Triple Fruit Flambé, 73
Cherry Tomatoes and Shrimp in
  Herb Butter, 17
Chicken
  Breasts Mère Catherine, 63
  Cashew, 61
  in Casserole with Grapes, 64
  Glazed Breast of, with
    Grapes, 61
  -Mushroom Fondue, 35
  Normandy, 62
Chicken Livers in Cream, 62
Chile, green
  Ajoqueso, 13
  and Cheese Dip, 12
Chile Sauce, Spicy, 39
Chive and Crab Filling, for
  pancakes, 21
Chutney
  Sauce, 42
  Tomato Lemon, 43
Clam
  Dip, Hot, 12
  and Sausage Appetizers, 14
Cocktail Sauce, 39
Cold Blender Béarnaise, 38
Confetti Eggs, 52
Convertible burners, 6, 7
Crab
  -Egg Scramble, Creamy, 50
  -Filled Brunch Pancakes, 65
  Filling, for pancakes, 21

Creamy Crab-Egg Scramble, 50
Crêpes
  Brittany, 79
  Brittany, with Ice Cream,
    Flambé, 79
  Butter Cream, with Jam, 77
  Café Au Lait, 77
  Caramel Pear, 78
  French, 76-78
  Ice Cream with Flaming
    Blueberry Sauce, 77
  Orange, 76
  Strawberry Ice Cream, 78
Crêpes Suzette Pan, 5
Curried
  Eggs with Avocado, 51
  Mushroom Filling, for
    pancakes, 21
Curry
  Dip, 45
  Mayonnaise, Blender, 40
  Sauce, for meatballs, 58

Dessert Fondue Sauces, 74-75
Desserts, 66-79
Dieter's Gourmet Sauce, 41
Dipping Kettle, 17
Dips
  Curry, 45
  Green Chile and Cheese, 12
  Hot Clam, 12
  Smoked Cheese, for pears
    and apples, 19

Earthenware fondue pot, 5, 7
Eggs
  for Aïoli, 19
  Confetti, 52
  Curried, with Avocado, 51
  Fried with Prawns and Dill, 51
  Nut-Crusted Oysters and, 49
  Omelet, 53-54
  Rancheros, 50
  Scrambled, with crab, 50
  Scrambled, with ham, 52
  Scrambled, and Smoked
    Salmon on Toast, 49
  Tomatoes and, Italian, 50
  Tortillas Con Hongos, 52
Electric fondue pots, 6, 7
Equipment, 5-6, 7, 8, 24, 28-29,
  47-48
  care of, 8-9
  safety, 9

Fettucine, 60
Figs
  Butter Rum, 71
  Stuffed, in Wine Sauce, 69
Fillings
  Crab and Chive, for
    pancakes, 21
  Curried Mushroom, for
    pancakes, 21
Fish, See also individual kinds
  for Aïoli, 19
  Seafood Fondue, 31;
    photograph, 22
Flaming
  Dessert Bananas, 68
  procedure for, 8
  Shrimp, 17
Fondue, 22-35
  Ajoqueso, 13
  Bourguignonne, 23, 30
  Broth, 33-35
  Brunch Swiss, 26
  Burnt-Sugar, 75
  Butterscotch, 74
  Cheese, 24
  Cherries Jubilee, 68
  Chicken-Mushroom, 35
  Dessert Sauces, 74-75
  Fonduta, 27
  Lamb, 31
  Mizutaki, 34-35
  oil, 28-32
  Orange-Honey, 75
  Poached Seafood and
    Vegetables, 33
  Powdered Sugar, 74
  Salami and Cheese, 13;
    photograph, 10
  Seafood, 31; photograph 22
  Seafood-Vegetable Tempura,
    32
  Shrimp, 27
  Swiss, 24-25
  Swiss Cheese Dipping Sauce,
    26
  Swiss Chocolate, 75
Fonduta, 27
French Crêpes, 76-78
Fuels, 6-8
  safety, 9

Garlic Pork Nuggets, 13
Glazed Breast of Chicken with
  Grapes, 61
Grapes
  with chicken casserole, 64
  with glazed breast of
    chicken, 61
  in Triple Fruit Flambé, 73

Green Chile
  Ajoqueso, 13
  and Cheese Dip, 12
Guacamole, 41

Ham and Scrambled Eggs, 52
Herb Butter, for cherry tomatoes
  and shrimp, 17
Hollandaise Sauce
  Blender, 40
  Mousseline, 40
Honey-Chocolate Sundae Sauce,
  72
Horseradish sauces, 42
Hot Caramel Peaches, 70
Hot Clam Dip, 12

Ice Cream
  with Brittany Crêpes, 79
  Crêpes with Flaming
    Blueberry Sauce, 77
  Crêpes, with strawberries, 78
  Mold with Flaming Nut
    Sauce, 70

Joe's Special, 57

Lamb Fondue, 31
Lemon
  Basting Sauce, 64
  Mayonnaise Sauce, 40
  Tomato Chutney, 43
Lobster
  for Aïoli, 19
  La Flamberge, 53

Mandarin Oranges
  Flambé, 72
  in Triple Fruit Flambé, 73
Mayonnaise
  Blender Curry, 40
  Lemon Sauce, 40
  Pesto, 44
Meatballs
  Appetizer, 20
  Baked, and Variations, 58-59
  with Curry Sauce, 58
  Sauerbraten, 59
  Spicy, 21
  in Wine Sauce, 58
Mizutaki, 34-35
Mock Béarnaise Sauce, 38
Mushrooms
  Bourguignonne, 16
  Bruncheon, 55
  -Cashew Medley, 54
  Chicken Fondue, 35
  Curried, filling for pancakes,
    21
  and Shrimp Sauté, 65

Nut-Crusted Oysters and Eggs,
  49

Oil Fondue, 28-32
Omelet, 53-54
Orange Crêpes, 76
Orange-Honey Fondue, 75
Oysters and eggs, 49

Pancakes, see also Crêpes
  Appetizer, 20-21
  Crab-Filled Brunch, 65
Pasta
  Fettucine, 60
Peaches
  Fire and Ice, 69
  Hot Caramel, 70
  in Hot Melba Sauce, 71
  and Rum Babas, 70
Pears
  and Apples with Smoked
    Cheese Dip, 19
  Crêpes, Caramel, 78
Pesto, 44
  Butter, 44
  Mayonnaise, 44
  Sauce, 44
Poached Seafood and
  Vegetables, 33
Pork, Garlic Nuggets, 13
Powdered Sugar Fondue, 74
Praline Sundae Sauce, 71
Prawns, with fried eggs, 51

Quick Sukiyaki, 55

Red Wine Sauce, 45
Rémoulade Sauce, 42
Restaurant units, 6
Rice, wild, with beef medallions
  sauté, 56

Safety, 9
Salami and Cheese Fondue, 13;
  photograph, 10
Salmon
  Fillets Flambé, 64
  Smoked, and Scrambled Eggs
    on Toast, 49
Sauces, 36-45
  Aïoli, 18
  Almond, for scallops, 65

Anchovy, 39
Avocado, 41
Bagna Cauda, 15
Béarnaise, for chicken, 63
Blender Béarnaise, 38
Blender Curry Mayonnaise, 40
Blender Hollandaise, 40
Buttermilk Cheese, 26
Chutney, 42
Cocktail, 39
Cold Blender Béarnaise, 38
Curry Dip, 45
Dessert Fondue, 74-75
Dieter's Gourmet, 41
Dill, 14
Flaming Blueberry, for ice
  cream crêpes, 77
Flaming Nut, for ice cream
  mold, 70
Flavored Butters, 43
Guacamole, 41
Honey-Chocolate Sundae, 72
Horseradish, 42
Hot Melba, 71
Lemon Basting, 64
Lemon Mayonnaise, 40
Mizutaki, 35
Mock Béarnaise, 38
Mousseline, 40
Newburg, 14
Pesto, 44
Praline Sundae, 71
Red Wine, 45
Rémoulade, 42
Sour Cream, 38
Spicy Chile, 39
Swiss Cheese Dipping, 26
Tangy, for shrimp, 16
Tartar, 39
Tempura, 45
Teriyaki, 44
Tomato Lemon Chutney, 43
Whipped Horseradish Cream,
  42
Sausage and Clam Appetizers,
  14
Scallopini Picatte, 60
Scallops, Almond-Sauced, 65
Scrambled Eggs and Smoked
  Salmon on Toast, 49
Seafood, see also individual
  kinds
  Fondue, 31; photograph, 22
  Poached, and Vegetables, 33
  -Vegetable Tempura, 32
Sherried Shrimp with Tangy
  Sauce, 16
Shrimp
  for Aïoli, 19
  Cherry Tomatoes and, in
    Herb Butter, 17
  Chow Dun, 51
  Flaming, 17
  Fondue, 27
  and Mushroom Sauté, 65
  Sherried, 16
Sour Cream Sauce, 38
Spicy Chile Sauce, 39
Spicy Meatballs, 21
Steak
  Au Poivre, 56
  Diane, 57
Strawberries Fire and Ice, 69;
  photograph, 4
Strawberry Ice Cream Crêpes, 78
Stuffed Figs in Wine Sauce, 69
Sukiyaki, Quick, 55
Swiss
  Cheese Dipping Sauce, 26
  Chocolate Fondue, 75
  Fondue, 24-25
  Julienne of Veal, 59;
    photograph, 46

Tartar Sauce, 39
Tempura
  Sauce, 45
  Seafood-Vegetable, 32
Teriyaki Sauce, 44
Tomato Lemon Chutney, 43
Tomatoes
  Cherry, and Shrimp in Herb
    Butter, 17
  and Eggs Italian, 50
Tortillas Con Hongos, 52
Triple Fruit Flambé, 73

Veal
  Scallopini Picatte, 60
  Swiss Julienne of, 59;
    photograph, 46
Vegetables
  for Aïoli, 19
  for Bagna Cauda, 15
  for Mizutaki, 34-35
  and Poached Seafood, 33
  -Seafood Tempura, 32

Whipped Horseradish Cream
  Sauce, 42

Zabaglione, 73